THE ADAPTIVE INVESTMENT PORTFOLIO

THE ADAPTIVE INVESTMENT PORTFOLIO

A SMARTER, MORE DYNAMIC WAY TO INVEST IN ANY MARKET CYCLE

MICHAEL P. ERNST

ERNST & CO.
WEALTH MANAGEMENT, LLC.

Publishers Cataloging-in-Publication Data

Ernst, Michael P., 1967–
The adaptive investment portfolio™: a smarter more dynamic way to invest in any market cycle / Michael P. Ernst.
p. cm.
ISBN: 978-1-7328946-0-0 (paperback)
[1. Wealth Management—Business & Economics. 2. Stocks—Business & Economics. 3. Portfolio Management—Business & Economics. 4. Financial Risk Management—Business & Economics. 5. Investing—Business & Economics. 6. Retirement Planning—Business & Economics. 7. Money Management—Business & Economics.] I. Title.

2018963263

Ernst & Co. Wealth Management, LLC
www.theadaptiveinvestmentportfolio.com

Second Edition
Printed and Bound in the United States of America

I DEDICATE THIS BOOK

to my beautiful wife, Jessica, and
our sons, Adam and Ethan, who are
a source of unlimited love, joy, and happiness.

TABLE OF CONTENTS

ACKNOWLEDGMENTS

Writing a book is harder than I imagined it would be and more rewarding as well. When I decided to publish my work and began to do the research on what it takes to get a manuscript completed and to print, I quickly realized I could not do it alone.

The idea for this book has been swirling around in my head for over two years. Thanks to a close group of family, friends, and colleagues I found the incredible support and encouragement needed to get the book out of my head and onto paper. I would like to extend my sincere thanks to my good friend, Chris Forest. Also, through numerous interviews and consultations, I was able to assemble an incredible team of professionals that I affectionately refer to as the "Delta Force" of book publishing.

I would like to thank my wife, Jessica, who is my true love and soul mate. Thank you for supporting my dream of writing this book during a very busy time in our lives and for the best eleven years of my life.

Thank you to my beautiful sons, Adam and Ethan, for the incredible joy and inspiration you bring. There is no experience in my life that has been more meaningful or more powerful than being your father.

To my "Delta Force" team: thank you for accepting the mission. A special thank you to John Waggoner for his help with the structure and organization of my manuscript and also for his valuable insight. My thanks and gratitude to Nancy Butts for her detailed editing work and for going the extra mile to make the publishing deadline. Also to Kathy Sparrow for her editing assistance, details matter. I am also very thankful and appreciative for the time, skill and creativity of Margaret Cogswell in the creation of my dust jacket, cover design, and book formatting.

INTRODUCTION

There is a push-pull situation in the economy that is making it increasingly important for investors to understand whether or not their portfolios are positioned for continued growth while also being prepared for economic uncertainty. This book is about how to improve the performance and the outcomes of your investments by enabling you to clearly see and understand the investment process and to approach it in a different way. You will gain a simple but deep understanding of the critical factors that affect financial markets and the primary factors that influence your investment behavior.

Investment strategies should be developed from a sound foundation of economic theory and a comprehensive investment philosophy. *The Adaptive Investment Portfolio* is a disciplined methodology with roots based in financial economics and academic research, one which investors can employ to enhance returns and mitigate losses. If you are looking for peace of mind and an alternative to conventional buy-and-hold stock strategies, this book is for you.

If you watch the financial news, you've probably noticed that for every pundit predicting a crash, there's another who claims the stock market will go through the roof. Both of these pundits are appealing to the two most basic tenets of human behavior: the desire to avoid pain and pursue pleasure. Typically, it is these two emotions, and not logic, that drive investment behavior.

Interestingly, when we compare these two basic principles, we find that our desire to avoid pain is much stronger than our desire to pursue pleasure. Furthermore, it is the perception of pain and pleasure, not actual pain and pleasure, that drives people to act irrationally at market tops and bottoms. Since we don't know for sure what the future will hold, our brain is constantly making assumptions and judgments about what may happen. Unfortunately, many times those assumptions are flawed, especially when it comes to more complex matters, such as our approach to investing.

For example, while we all know intellectually that we should buy low and sell high, the fear of loss and the pursuit of gains may cause us to do just the opposite. At market tops, FOMO—fear of missing out—causes many investors to add more risk to their portfolios, usually just in time for a new market cycle downturn. When stocks are cheap and beaten down, the fear of further losses causes investors to avoid buying. When we think about it logically, it's like saying, "Gosh! This new car at 10 percent below list price is just too darn cheap. I'm going to wait until it's really overpriced before I hop in the driver's seat."

We want the pleasure of watching our money grow and, at the same time, we want to avoid the pain of watching our investments lose value as markets go down. What makes us obey our basic pain and pleasure principles, rather than our common sense? The most common missing ingredient is conviction—which is essential to staying the course. When we do not know exactly what our portfolio is invested in or why, we lack the required conviction and get shaken out of the market when it becomes volatile. Life being the way it is, this typically happens at or near the market bottom—the worst possible time.

How do we avoid taking an emotional response to managing our portfolios in an environment of market uncertainty? After all, we are now living in rapidly-changing times: everything from an unconventional U.S. president to trade wars, geopolitical unpredictability, and shifting central bank policy creates uncertainty that can shake investor confidence.

In this book, we will also examine one of the most hotly-debated topics in finance, active vs. passive investing. Is it better to have an active fund manager, or simply track an index? The proponents of each side have dug in deep and seem unwilling to give up even an inch of ground when discussing which is better for investors. While there are strong arguments to be made for both, the fact is that the performance of active and passive management has been cyclical, with each approach alternating periods of outperformance with one another. This book will show you how to benefit from the best of what each has to offer.

Our journey together would be incomplete without an examination of the stock and bond markets and market cycles, and the effect they have on passive investing, active investing, and our behavior. I believe you will have an *"ah ha!"* moment as these pieces come together and you gain a clear understanding of how and why *The Adaptive Investment Portfolio* can insulate you and your portfolio from the unpredictability of ever-changing markets.

In order to be a successful investor, you need a dynamic portfolio that adapts to rapidly-evolving market circumstances. *The Adaptive Investment Portfolio* fills the gaps that are left by other books on the subject and offers an easy-to-understand approach that simplifies what is too often overly complex. This book shares how and why the Adaptive Investment Portfolio is a superior way to approach investing and offers a clear and defined process that outlines the steps you can take to seize control of your emotions and your future.

In all market environments, one can identify reasons for optimism and reasons for concern. We don't want to necessarily speculate in favor of one or the other (trading vs. investing); rather, we want to invest for both possible outcomes. This requires the discipline, patience, and conviction that is granted by a methodical and measured approach. The Adaptive Investment Portfolio provides just that.

CHAPTER 1

WHAT DRIVES OUR DECISIONS: REASON OR EMOTION?

Nature has placed mankind under the governance of two sovereign masters, pain and pleasure.
- Epicurus, 300 BC

We make decisions every single day, all day, from the moment we wake up until the second we lay our heads on a pillow. What will I eat for breakfast? What clothes do I wear today? Which way will I drive to work? All of these decisions can be made with a mix of emotion and reason. When we make decisions about money, however, reason has to rule—and that's why you need a rules-based system for investing that will keep a rein on your emotions.

For most people, however, emotions rule investment decisions. Why? From the time of our birth, we build an emotional database of past experiences and actions. These experiences guide our own internal navigation system—our gut feelings—that direct our decisions. The question is how much this emotional database helps or hinders our decision-making.

One of the primary conventions of financial theory holds that participants in an economy are essentially rational "wealth maximizers," meaning that they will make decisions based on the information around them in a way that is as reasonable as possible. However, in actuality there are countless instances in which emotion has an undue influence over our decisions. The result, is that so-called "rational" people can display unpredictable or irrational behaviors. Whether we experience the feelings of love, anger, happiness, sadness, greed, or fear, we are all capable of making deeply silly or irrational decisions when emotions are the main driver in the decision-making process.

My wife, Jessica, will be the first to admit she is inexplicably obsessed with shoes. Talk about pain and pleasure: the purchase of fabulous shoes makes her feel great, but they just can't be comfortable! I once made a comment about how painful her high heels looked and she said to me, "The higher the heel, the better you feel," explaining to me that a great shoe can completely transform your outfit and your mood. How can I argue with that perceptive psychological insight? My wife is not only beautiful on the inside and out, she is also smart—and always well put-together. The companies selling these shoes know all about the compelling emotional response these shoes generate and fully capitalize on it. With billions of dollars on the line, advertising companies have devised marketing campaigns that are designed to motivate people to buy based on psychological triggers like these. Carrie Bradshaw from *Sex in the City*, with her closet full of Manolo Blahniks, Jimmy Choos, and Louboutins, only helped drive my wife's proclivity for buying shoes.

Now the question to be asked is: Do investors make rational or emotional decisions? The answer is both. The relatively new field of behavioral economics questions the conventional assumption that investors are rational and suggests the notion that they act emotionally and are therefore prone to making mistakes. Understanding how we as individual investors process information and manage our emotions can help us to construct better investment portfolios and ultimately achieve an overall better investment outcome.

> *Investing isn't about beating others at their game.*
> *It's about controlling yourself at your own game.*
>
> *Benjamin Graham*

Here's an example of how behavioral economics works: I always hear the argument that if you simply stay in the market it will eventually recover, which is mostly true (except in Japan, where the Nikkei 225 Index, a benchmark index for the country, peaked in 1989). The problem is that investors simply do not have the mindset to hold on in times of crisis and through extreme market fluctuations. A December 2015 Ned Davis research study showed that the average retail investor now holds stocks and/or mutual funds for less than one year, which is simply too short a time frame to deal with a full market cycle and to meet your investment goals. Despite the frequent recommendations you hear in the news about investing for the long term, the reality is that most people don't do that. Investor psychology is the reason why.

It is not just the Ned Davis Research study but my own experience over almost twenty-five years that confirms this behavior of the average investor. As part of my client discovery process, I ask clients a variety of questions in order to gauge the individual's tolerance for risk and their ability to endure the up and down movements of market cycles. As an example, in the section of my questionnaire on market participation, I ask these three questions:

1. Global markets, though volatile, have historically been great engines of long-term wealth creation, and a portion of my

portfolio should be exposed to the returns and volatility associated with these markets: Yes or No?

2. Would you expect some portion of your portfolio to be actively managed during periods of market volatility, the goal being to create an improved risk adjusted return? Yes or No?
3. Do you want some portion of your portfolio not subject to market movement, especially during periods of sustained market declines? Yes or No?

The overwhelming majority of those taking the questionnaire answer yes to all three of the above questions. They certainly do want to participate to the greatest extent possible in the wealth-creation capabilities of the markets, but that exposure must match their tolerance for market turbulence. Simultaneously, the majority of questionnaire participants expect a portion of their portfolios to be actively managed during periods of market volatility. Nearly 100 percent of those taking the questionnaire want some portion of their portfolios out of the market during periods of sustained market declines. I can tell you right now that the first place many investors turn during a financial crisis is to their financial advisor. When the markets are not doing well or they are totally tanking, it is absolutely necessary to know that your investment plan matches your personal sensitivity to the markets. This preparation must be done in advance, and you must be able to adapt.

The Ned Davis research findings are backed up by numerous other studies. One of them is the 24th annual quantitative analysis of investor behavior by Dalbar[1], released in December of 2017.

[1] Dalbar, Inc. is the financial community's leading independent expert for evaluating, auditing and rating business practices, customer performance, product quality and service.

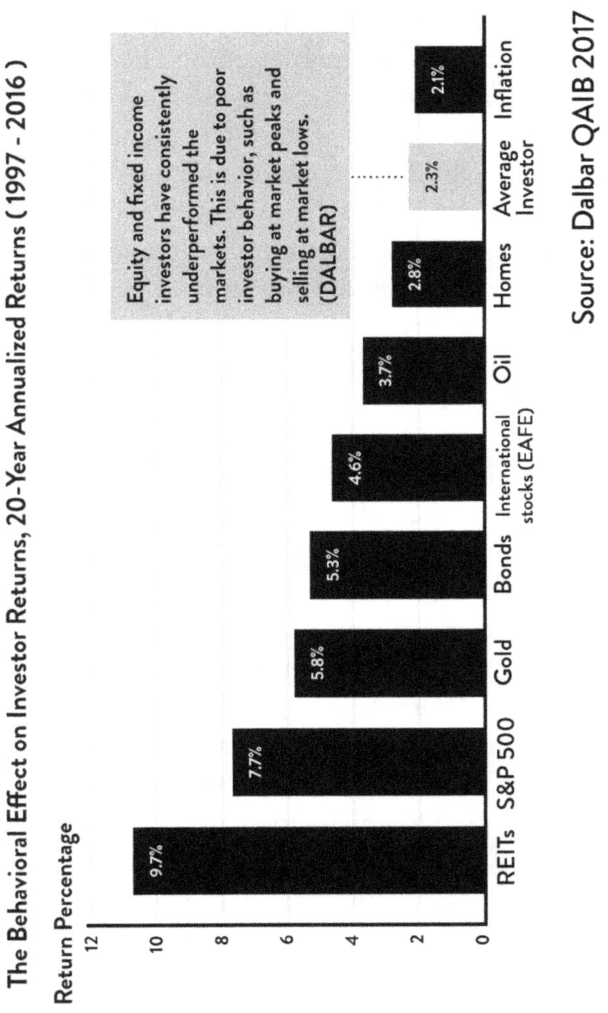
The Behavioral Effect on Investor Returns, 20-Year Annualized Returns (1997 - 2016)
Return Percentage
12
10
8
6
4
2
0
9.7%
7.7%
5.8%
5.3%
4.6%
3.7%
2.8%
2.3%
2.1%
REITs
S&P 500
Gold
Bonds
International stocks (EAFE)
Oil
Homes
Average Investor
Inflation
Equity and fixed income investors have consistently underperformed the markets. This is due to poor investor behavior, such as buying at market peaks and selling at market lows. (DALBAR)
Source: Dalbar QAIB 2017

Figure 1.[2]

[2] Ibid.

The study examines investor returns in equity, fixed income, and asset allocation funds. The analysis covers the thirty-year period ending Dec, 31, 2017, encompassing the recovery from the crash of 1987, the drop at the turn of the millennium, the crash of 2008, the recovery from the 2008 recession, and the bull market leading up to today. No matter what the current state of the mutual fund industry is, boom or bust, investment results are more dependent on investor behavior than they are on fund performance. Dalbar defined nine of the irrational investment behavior biases.

1. **Loss aversion**: Fearing loss leads to a withdrawal of capital at the worst possible time. Wonder who all those people are who sell during big market downturns? Look in the mirror—or at your mutual fund manager. A less polite term for "loss aversion" is "panic selling."
2. **Narrow framing**: Making decisions about one part of the portfolio without considering the effects on the total. The market is hot, so you sell your stodgy bond fund for a red-hot growth fund. When the growth fund walks off a cliff, you no longer have the bond fund to buffer the fall.
3. **Anchoring**: Remaining focused on what happened previously and not adapting to a changing market. Those who had great returns on Freddie Mac and Fannie Mae, the quasi-governmental mortgage giants, often refused to believe that those companies' days as growth stocks were long gone.
4. **Mental accounting**: Separating performance of investments mentally to justify success and failure.
5. **Lack of diversification**: Believing a portfolio is diversified when in fact it is a highly correlated pool of assets. Most people remember their winners, but downplay their losers. It's the combination of the two that determines your outcome.

6. **Herding**: Following what everyone else is doing. This leads to the "buy high/sell low" error. You probably knew people who wouldn't shut up about their investments in technology in 2000 or Bitcoin in 2017—and those people probably convinced lots of other people to follow them. Not surprisingly, you didn't hear much from them when the market fell apart.
7. **Regret**: Not performing a necessary action due to the regret of a previous failure. You sold Apple in 2011 when Steve Jobs died. Bad call! So when General Electric tumbled 47 percent in 2017, you held on. That was probably a bad call, too.
8. **Media response**: Responding to the media bias towards optimism and its effort to sell products from advertisers and attract viewers or readers. If you're looking for a long-term investment, a daily stock trading show is probably not the place to find it.
9. **Optimism**: Making overly optimistic assumptions that tend to lead to dramatic reversals when met with reality. We all like to think the best of the future, but rose-colored glasses don't help our investment outlook. The University of Michigan's Consumer Sentiment Survey often hits its biggest peak just before the stock market turns down[3].

There is a tenth and final factor as well: overconfidence. Psychologists have found that humans tend to have unwarranted confidence in their decision-making process. We have an inflated view of our own abilities, typically greater than reality warrants. This trait appears to be universal. Researchers have asked people to rate their own abilities, and found that most of us are woefully

[3] Roberts, Lance. "The Money Game & The Human Brain." *Real Investment Advice.* 10 September 2018. https://realinvestmentadvice.com/the-money-game-the-human-brain/ Accessed 13 October 2018.

overconfident. For example, take a person who thinks he is invaluable to his employer when there are plenty of qualified people who could do his job. This person may show his overconfidence by coming in late to work because he thinks he is never going to get fired, or by being overly demanding about getting a raise.

When it comes to our money and investments, we run into problems when we turn out to be right for the wrong reasons, confusing luck with ability. This is when things can go to your head, and you start feeling that you are invincible and can do no wrong. Nassim Taleb, famed risk analyst, made this analogy about being fooled by randomness.

> Reality is far more vicious than Russian roulette. First, it delivers the fatal bullet rather infrequently, like a revolver that would have hundreds, even thousands of chambers instead of six. After a few dozen tries, one forgets about the existence of a bullet, under a numbing false sense of security. Second, unlike a well-defined precise game like Russian roulette, where the risks are visible to anyone capable of multiplying and dividing by six, one does not observe the barrel of reality. One is capable of unwittingly playing Russian roulette—and calling it by some alternative "low risk" game.[4]

Jesse Livermore (July 26, 1877—November 28, 1940) was an American investor and securities analyst who gained notoriety for making and losing several multimillion-dollar fortunes and

---

[4] Taleb, Nassim M., *Fooled By Randomness, The Hidden Role of Chance in the Markets and in Life.* Texerre, LLC., 2001.

short selling[5] during the stock market crashes in 1907 and 1929. Livermore, one of the greatest stock traders of all time, understood that self-mastery leads to market mastery. Livermore said, "The human side of every person is the greatest enemy of the average investor or speculator." He added, "Fear keeps you from making as much money as you ought to. Wishful thinking must be banished."[6]

In practical terms, human beings tend to view the world in a positive light. While this behavior can be valuable, as it can help you recover from life's disappointments more quickly, it can also cause an ongoing source of bias in money-related decisions.

For most people, emotional flaws combine to create double or triple whammies. Consider the combination of the herding effect and loss aversion which tend to work in tandem, compounding investor's mistakes. As markets rise, individuals are led to think that rising prices will last indefinitely. The four most dangerous words in investing are, "This time it's different." The longer that prices continue to rise, the more strongly investors believe in the trend until the very last holdouts buy in and the market becomes euphoric. As markets eventually decline, as they always do, there is a slow realization that this decline is more than an opportunity to "buy the dip," as it has been in the past. As losses continue to mount, and the anxiety of the loss becomes acute, the investor seeks to avert further loss—and pain—by selling. The nineteenth-century British writer Oscar Wilde once shared the pithy aphorism, "Man is a rational animal who always loses his temper when he is called upon to act in accordance with the dictates of reason."

---

[5] Short selling is the sale of a security that is not owned by the seller or that the seller has borrowed. Short selling is motivated by the belief that a security's price will decline, enabling it to be bought back at a lower price to make a profit.

[6] Lefevre, Edwin. *Reminiscences of a Stock Operator*. Originally published in 1923 by George H. Doran Company. Traders Press, Inc., 1985.

Case after case consistently tells us that humans do not behave rationally very often, but are driven by bias and biology. No less a genius, Sir Isaac Newton was susceptible to emotion-driven investing. Newton was sucked into buying shares of the South Sea Company of 1720. In a clever ploy to reduce its debt, the British government allowed investors to swap government debt for shares in the South Seas Company, to which it granted a monopoly on business operations in South America. This was an empty gesture, since the government had precious few business operations in South America. Nevertheless, the shares were wildly popular and soared to extravagant heights. Newton could not resist.

A depiction of the story can be found in Benjamin Graham's 1949 classic, *The Intelligent Investor*, which attributes the irrationality of market systems to the human-like qualities of an entity named "Mr. Market Investor."

> Back in the spring of 1720, Sir Isaac Newton owned shares in the South Sea Company, the hottest stock in England. Sensing that the market was getting out of hand, the great physicist muttered that he "could calculate the motions of the heavenly bodies, but not the madness of the people." Newton dumped his South Sea shares, pocketing a percent profit totaling £7,000. But just months later, swept up in the wild enthusiasm of the market, Newton jumped back in at a much higher price—and lost 20,000 pounds or more than $3 million in [2002-2003's] today's money. For the rest of his life, he forbade anyone to speak the words "South Sea" in his presence.

It seems that Newton, Britain's most celebrated mathematician, once a prudent investor who was known to spread his money across multiple securities, had been stricken by the euphoria of markets and plunged essentially all of his money into a single stock.

Although there are many stories of asset manias and bubbles and the wreckage they leave behind, the most recent is perhaps the most epic of all. Of course, I am talking about Bitcoin. Bitcoin is the decentralized, peer-to-peer cryptocurrency that was introduced in 2009 by a mysterious figure named Satoshi Nakamoto, whose true identity is still unknown to this day. (I know, it sounds like a story right out of the movies. I am sure there is one in the works.) Unlike a traditional currency, Bitcoin is not something you can see or hold in your hand. It is not issued or supported by a country, government, or central bank. The Bitcoin system is designed to allow online users to process transactions digitally through cryptocurrency exchanges.

Thus the coins are virtual; that is, they exist only electronically and are stored in a digital wallet in the cloud or on your computer. They can be either "mined" by computers through a process of solving a set of complex mathematical algorithms, or bought online. In the latter case, Bitcoins are purchased with standard currency such as the U.S. dollar or the euro. Bitcoin can be bought and sold in places like the San Francisco exchange, Coinbase.

Bitcoin has a limited supply of 21 million coins, of which about 17 million are in circulation. Bitcoin payments are processed through a private network of computers linked through a shared program. Each Bitcoin transaction is simultaneously recorded in a "blockchain" ledger on each computer that updates and informs all accounts. Bitcoin purchases are private, and there are no third-party intermediaries like governments or banks to interrupt a transaction.

The price appreciation of each Bitcoin has been extraordinary and is the definition of a bubble, a mania, and a crash all in one.

Bitcoin's first big move was in 2010, when it soared 900 percent, going from $0.008 to $0.08 in just a five-day period. This was the takeoff: early adopters were hooked. Indeed, some "Bitcoin millionaires" scored extreme profits, but many other investors who got caught up in the hype experienced devastating losses.

On a tip from some of his work friends at a Silicon Valley technology company, one early investor I'll call John Johnson (his name has been changed to protect his privacy) invested $3,000 late in 2010 to purchase 20,000 Bitcoin when the price was just over $0.15 per coin. The price movements were fairly steady as Johnson checked the value of his investment every few months or so. He did know early on that it was highly speculative; his plan was to just keep the Bitcoins and see what would happen. He was in it for the long haul.

Over the next three years, Johnson continued to work his regular job and had nearly forgotten about his speculative bet, until the price of Bitcoin started to really move and caught the attention of the mainstream media in 2013. The price continued to increase by 10 percent or more just about every day. Johnson was exhilarated and terrified all at once. The price hit $350, his original investment of $3,000 appreciating by more than 2,000 times. Then two days later, it rocketed to $800 per coin.

This rapid price appreciation really captured media attention. Meanwhile, Johnson had been selling off coins to take his profits along the way, and ultimately experienced a windfall of over $25 million. Stories like this got people talking; he and the other lucky ones who experienced the same ride to riches came to be known as "Bitcoin millionaires." Enthusiasm, greed, delusion, and calls for a "new paradigm" were all neatly in place. (Remember the fallacy, "This time it's different!") The price ultimately hit a high of $20,500 on Dec. 18, 2017, sucking in legions of would-be millionaires along the way. On that same day when Bitcoin hit the record high price, it had fluctuated up and down wildly, trading as low as $18,170 before it finally settled that day at a closing price of $19,055.

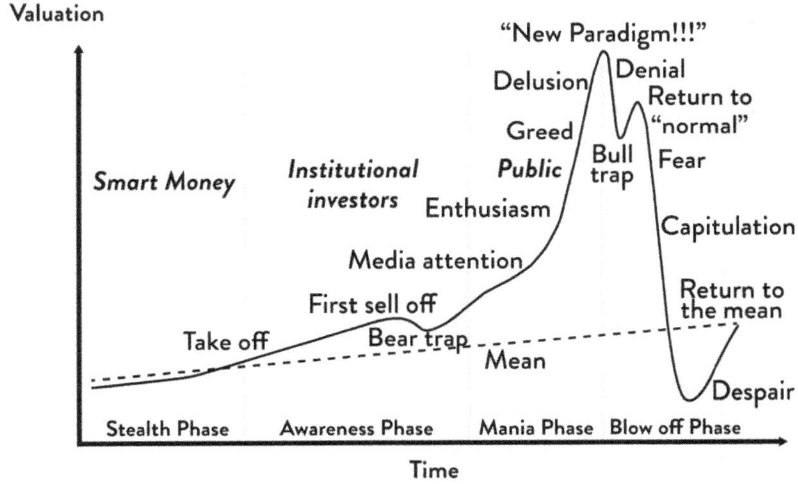

Figure 2. At market bottoms, some investors will tend to become overly risk averse and miss out on the start of a new bull market cycle. These mistakes can be avoided when investors seek professional investment guidance to protect against the natural tendencies that are so common.

The point at which we enter an investment fixes in our minds a reference point against which we judge future gains or losses. Bitcoin investors who entered at or near these market tops, had a great deal of large losses in their futures. Since we are so averse to losses, many investors were in denial as the bad news for the cryptocurrency started to pile up and price declines continued to gain speed. Nevertheless, news about Bitcoin's astonishing appreciation and the riches experienced by some continued to spread. The fear of missing out (FOMO) for many is a powerful emotion, and the get-rich-quick crowd simply could not resist the tantalizing opportunity to participate in this golden opportunity. They believed the new technology would surely recast the way we all look at money and revolutionize both finance and the world. Additionally, the visionaries proclaimed that cryptocurrency technology would follow in the Internet's disruptive footsteps.

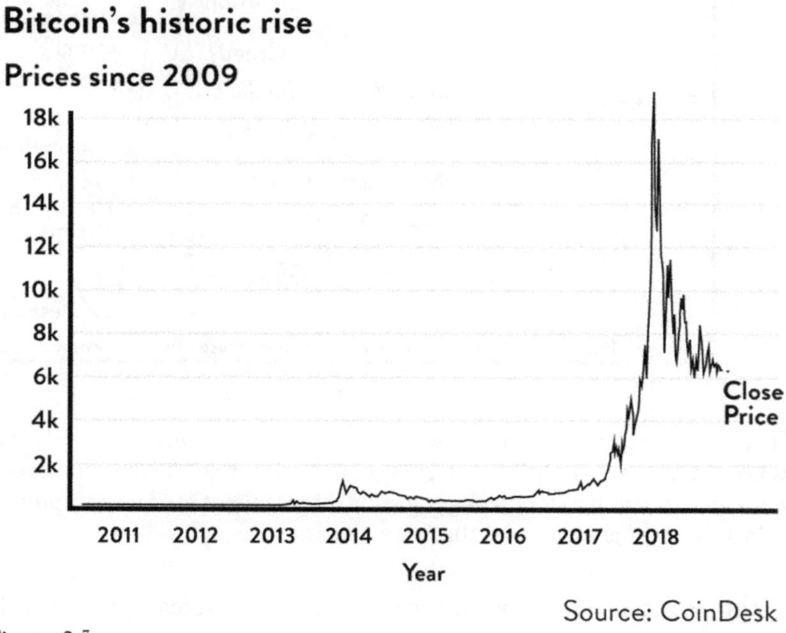

Figure 3.[7]

What Bitcoin enthusiasts overlooked, however, was that it was fairly easy to create other new cryptocurrencies as well. At the

[7] Rooney, Kate. "Bitcoin turns 10 — how it went from an abstract idea to a $100 billion market in a decade." CNBC.com. 31 October 2018. https://www.cnbc.com/2018/10/31/bitcoin-turns-10-years-old.html. Accessed 31 October 2018.

moment, there are more than 1,000. They also overlooked the fact that the price of Bitcoin and its imitators, like penny stocks, are extremely easy to manipulate. And that total privacy feature? It's not completely private when thousands of computers contain records of every transaction. If the FBI—or criminals—can crack your digital wallet, you may not only lose all your money, but wind up in jail, too.

Bitcoin continued to trade lower through the end of December 2017, bottoming out at $11,300 before taking a bounce: the kind that is often called a "bull trap." This is a false indication that a declining trend in a stock (or Bitcoin) has reversed and is heading upwards when, in fact, the security will ultimately continue to decline. It is aptly named because it sucks in and traps those with a bullish view that a security is going higher. But I digress.

As the price attempted a continued recovery for a period of about six weeks, finally getting back to as high as $16,790, many cryptocurrency enthusiasts were relieved to see a return to "normal" and expected the value to go much higher. New projections for prices as high as $150,000 or more sucked in more believers. The day after hitting $16,790, Bitcoin traded down to a low of $13,960 before finally closing that day at $14,970. It has been trending lower ever since then. As of the writing of this book, Bitcoin is trading in the $6,000 range and has seen a low of $5,755—this is down over 70 percent from its high of $20,500.

What has followed the euphoria is fear, capitulation, and despair. Although the price is still in the stratosphere compared to the starting price of $0.008, many would-be Bitcoin millionaires have been financially ruined. Some of those who got caught up in the excitement, fearful of missing out, maxed out their credit cards, took out personal loans, and even refinanced homes to get in on the Bitcoin action. The stories are plentiful and all equally devastating.

As the sad saga of Bitcoin illustrates, the neurology of pain and pleasure, as well as the psychology of fear and greed, are key drivers of our financial behavior. Groundbreaking developments in the field of neuroscience in the last decade have provided surprising insights into how the brain really works. We can now see in real time how blood, oxygen, and neurons behave, activating various parts of the brain. Thanks to science, we can watch the brain's decision-making process at work. And scientists, teaming up with economists, have made some surprising discoveries about how we make financial decisions.

Far from being coldly rational people who act in our own best interests—the basis for classic economic theory—behavioral economics looks at the effects of psychological, cognitive, emotional, cultural, and social factors which make us human and often lead us to deeply-flawed decisions. The central assumption of the theory is that losses and disadvantages have greater impact on our decisions than do gains and advantages. People tend to prefer the avoidance of losses over the acquisitions of gains. It is better to not lose five dollars than to find the same amount.[8] Some estimates suggest people weigh losses more than twice as heavily as potential gains. As such, the field of behavioral economics maintains a primary focus on the bounds of rationality in decision making. Behavioral models typically integrate microeconomic theory with the insight from psychology that greed and fear motivate us, and the insight from neurology that the avoidance of pain and the maximization

[8] Tversky, Amos and Daniel Kanhamn. "Loss Aversion in Riskless Choice: A Reference Dependent Model." *The Quarterly Journal of Economics*," vol. 106, no. 4, 1991, pp. 1039-1061. http://www.jstor.org/stable/2937956. Accessed 12 October. 2018.

of pleasure are what drive financial decisions. [9]

Investing without emotion is easier said than done, particularly because of the uncertainty of markets. So how is an investor to remove the emotion from investing and increase the probability of a positive outcome? Understanding your emotional tolerance for risk is essential to staying the course. Conviction can make the difference between your investment portfolio being decimated or having it be extremely profitable over time.

For example, significant declines are a normal part of market fluctuations. History has shown that markets will experience years when stocks go down 20, 30, and even 40 percent or more, and it can test an investor's conviction and the will to resist selling. As we have discussed, research has shown that investors tend to panic sell at market bottoms, causing them to miss out on the following recovery.

As an example, the financial crisis of 2007-2008 is considered by many economists to have been the worst financial crisis since the Great Depression of the 1930s, and legions of terrified investors sold in fear, realizing devastating losses. The U.S. stock market peaked on October 9, 2007, when the Dow Jones Industrial Average closed at an all-time high of 14,164.53 points. There was a complete evaporation of liquidity and the Dow entered a pronounced decline, ultimately falling more than 50 percent. By March 9, 2009, the Dow Jones Industrial Average had reached a low of 6,547.05.

Investors were terrified and it is easy to understand why. *The Wall Street Journal* abandoned its usual cool demeanor to shout, "Mounting Fears Shake World Markets As Banking Giants Rush to Raise Capital." *WSJ* brandished the word "crisis" in two other

---

[9] Minton, Elizabeth A; Kahle, Lynn R. *Belief Systems, Religion, and Behavioral Economics: Marketing in Multicultural Environments.* Business Expert Press, 2013.

headlines: "Crisis on Wall Street as Lehman Totters, Merrill is Sold, AIG Seeks to raise cash" and "U.S. Drafts Sweeping Plan to Fight Crisis As Turmoil Worsens in Credit Markets." Meanwhile, *The New York Times* talked about investors running to safety, and *The Washington Post* said, "Markets in Disarray as Lending Locks Up."

You get the picture: scary stuff if you are not braced for it. If you were emotionally prepared—and had a plan—you would have weathered the market storm. Just four years later, the Dow hit an all-time record high. But, it is difficult to make fully rational financial decisions for most investors in normal times, much less in the middle of a market crisis. Because none of us can predict the future, and because markets are uncertain by nature, successful investing requires careful planning and discipline. The plan includes having a portfolio that assumes worst-case scenarios could potentially happen and is simultaneously designed for best-case scenarios. You should not make your decisions based on fear.

Investors must have the ability to override emotional triggers and the automatic response to them. First, you must establish decision-based rules for extreme market scenarios when you are building the portfolio, not in the middle of a market crisis. The next chapters will outline those rules. Jesse Livermore believed that the non-rational element of investor activity was the main driver in the repetition of price trends and patterns. "There is nothing new on Wall Street or in stock speculation…this is because human nature does not change, and it is human emotion, solidly built into human nature, that always gets in the way of human intelligence. Of this I am sure."[10] I guess so. As someone who knew from personal experience how emotions can affect investing behavior, Livermore is a source of experiential wisdom.

Successful investing requires discipline, patience, and conviction!

---

[10] Lefevre, Edwin. *Reminiscences of a Stock Operator*. Originally published in 1923 by George H. Doran Company. Traders Press, Inc., 1985.

CHAPTER 2

UNDERSTANDING RISK

There is nothing riskier than the wide spread perception that there is not risk.
- Howard Marks

One way to moderate the effect of emotions on your investments is to have a solid understanding of your personal tolerance for risk—and a thorough understanding of what that actually is. The Adaptive Investment Portfolio is designed with your risk tolerance in mind and includes a built-in mechanism to manage that risk, allowing you to achieve your investment objectives with peace of mind.

Before you begin searching for the best investments that will help you reach your financial goals or have a professional investment advisor construct your portfolio, you have to understand your tolerance for investment risk, along with your goals, and time horizon. If you take on too much risk, you may be pushed out of your comfort zone, and your emotions will override your reason at critical junctures. But if you don't take enough risk, you might not earn enough to meet your goals—or even to overcome inflation.

Risk tolerance means the amount of market variability in investment returns that you are willing to withstand. Typically, your tolerance can be gauged by a questionnaire. Although I like to start with that, the best result is achieved when that is used in addition to a more personal one-on-one conversation and discovery process. The result will help to identify your investing style as aggressive, moderate, or conservative. A conservative investor won't be able to bear the ups and downs of a red hot biotechnology stock. An aggressive investor will be bored by a staid utility stock. Being invested in a portfolio that is too aggressive, could result in pulling the rip cord abruptly due to stock market fluctuations which does not typically serve an investor's goals, especially in the long run. I have clients that represent the full spectrum, and I cannot overemphasize the importance of having an investment portfolio that is constructed to meet your individual needs.

Here's an example of a question from a risk tolerance questionnaire.

What would you do if the stock market fell by 20 percent over the course of one year?

A. Buy more.
B. Wait a few months to make a decision.
C. Sell your stock positions immediately.

An aggressive investor would likely answer A, while a moderate investor would likely answer B, and a conservative investor would likely answer C.

When assessing your levels of risk tolerance, it is important to realize that all investments have some degree of risk; even the seemingly safe decision of putting your money into the bank carries potential perils of its own. This is because the value of your money may be eroded by inflation, which is currently heating up as the Federal Reserve has embarked on its cycle of interest rate hikes. There is also the opportunity cost of holding cash, which is the cost of the profit lost when choosing to hold the money rather than choosing to invest in another instrument that may provide a better return. Other risks include the possibility that you may get back less than your original investment. But, if you want to achieve significant levels of growth, you need to tolerate some levels of risk.

Constructing the right portfolio for you also involves a clear understanding of your risk capacity—that is, the amount of loss you can *afford* to take. This is different from the risk you are willing to take. If your tolerance for price fluctuations and your risk capacity are not in alignment with your investment portfolio, then it is unlikely that you will have the conviction or peace of mind that is required to stay the course and remain invested in the markets for the long term, thus keeping you on track and on target to reach your investment goals.

I had an appointment in my office with a prospective client who had a $2 million portfolio that she had been previously advised on by someone else. Prior to our meeting, she had completed the risk profile questionnaire I had given her, and she also sent over her most recent account statement for me to analyze. While we were in my office, we had a relaxed conversation about her goals and her plans for the future. In order to gather enough information to construct a personalized portfolio for her, I needed to have a deep understanding of what she was currently invested in, and what concerned her most in regard to her investments and eventual retirement.

As it turns out, she had inherited the portfolio from her husband who had passed away. She needed to invest in ways that would provide a steady stream of income. She was also worried about healthcare, because it was becoming higher on her list of expenses. She had never worked and was close to retirement age and the thought of the money running out was terrifying to her. She also had two young adult children whom she was helping with school and living expenses. She wanted to make sure that she could continue to assist with their futures as they built their own families. And she was worried about things she heard in the news and how they would affect her investments. Was there going to be war with North Korea or in the Middle East? How would trade tariffs with China affect her investments and her future? She did not feel prepared to get a job at her stage in life and did not have the ability to replace any of her money if lost.

On a scale of 1 to 100, with 1 being the most conservative and 100 being the most aggressive, this woman scored 18. After I had a chance to review her portfolio and do the analysis, I found that her portfolio had a corresponding risk score of 89. She had too much exposure to stocks and systemic market risk for both her level of risk tolerance and her age. She felt every up and down fluctuation in the market, and this left her constantly worried and uneasy.

My concern was that in the event of a market drawdown that was more severe and prolonged, she might not be able to endure the emotions associated with the potential losses and that she would be inclined to sell. Further, as we are late in the current expansion of the economic cycle, she would not be in an advantageous positions to wait it out in an effort to regain her losses. I was able to construct something more conservative and in line with her risk tolerance and that would also help her to reach her financial goals.

Her story provides a good illustration as to why you should develop a firm understanding of the relationship between your investment risk and your expected return in order to develop the required conviction for an investment position and to ensure the highest probability for long-term investment success. Most investors know that investing involves the possibility of loss, as well as potential for rewards. Generally speaking, the greater the market exposure, the greater the potential reward. While it is important to consider your personal exposure in the context of a specific investment or asset class, it is equally critical that investors consider market conditions.

Market risk refers to the chance of losses in the value of our investments due to changes in equity prices, interest rates, credit spreads, foreign-exchange rates, commodity prices, and other indicators of values that are set in the public markets. A more specific and academic definition of weighing risk would be what is called Mean-Variance Analysis—essentially the process of weighing risk, expressed as variance, against expected return.

Think of it this way. Large company stocks have returned 10.22 percent a year since 1926. That's the mean, or average. The worst yearly return was a 43.84 percent loss in 1931. (The second-worst year was 2008, which smacked investors for a 36.55 percent loss.) The best return was 52.56 percent in 1952, with 1933 coming in second, at 49.98 percent.

Naturally, investors tend to care most about variance from the mean when it's a loss; no one gripes about years with outsized gains. Nevertheless, investors use Mean-Variance Analysis to make decisions about which financial instruments to invest in, based on how much risk they are willing to take on in exchange for different levels of reward. Mean-Variance Analysis allows investors to find the biggest reward at a given level of risk or the least risk at a given level of return.[11]

---

[11] "Mean-Variance Analysis." *Investopedia*, https://www.investopedia.com/terms/m/mean-variance-analysis.asp. Accessed 12, October 2018.

Understanding your personal tolerance for risk along with your financial goals, objectives, and timeline are a critical part of this equation. Mean-variance analysis is one part of modern portfolio theory, which we will examine more closely in the next chapter. It assumes that investors will make rational decisions about their investments if they have complete information. The big question here is whether investors in general act or make decisions rationally, or whether they are more emotional.

Financial economists classify many different types of investment risk. Broadly speaking, this refers to the variability of outcomes; namely, how much you have gained or lost on your investment. Riskier investments should offer higher rates of return. Here are a few examples of the types of risk investors face:

Market Risk. Also known as systemic risk, this involves factors that affect the overall economy and/or securities markets the same way and cannot be mitigated by diversification. If there is a systemic crisis, the entire stock market may be affected and experience a sell-off, taking most, if not all, stocks down with it.

Interest Rate Risk. This is the possibility that an investment which pays regular income, such as a bond or preferred stock, will decline in value as a result of a rise in interest rates. Think of it this way—if you had a bond that yielded 5 percent, and rates on new bonds yielded 6 percent, other investors would turn up their noses at your measly 5 percent interest payment. You'd have to offer a discount on the bond's price to attract buyers. Whenever investors buy securities that offer a fixed rate of return, they are exposing themselves to interest-rate risk.

Credit Risk. When you buy a bond, you're a lender, and

credit ratings are as important for a bond as they are to a short-term loan to your shiftless Uncle Fred. Credit risk is the possibility that a company or bond issuer will not be able to make the interest rate payments or repay principal when the bond matures. It's also called default risk.

Liquidity Risk. This is the possibility that an investor may not be able to quickly buy or sell an investment, preventing the investor from turning the asset into cash. High-quality stocks are very liquid, because there are plenty of buyers and exchanges to facilitate the deal. Houses are not very liquid, because you need to deal with mortgage lenders, insurance companies, realtors, and other individuals to get the house sold. If you can't get an investment sold, it's worth little or nothing until a buyer emerges.

Inflation Risk. Inflation is the enemy of any investor. Suppose your swell Uncle Fred put $100 into a bank vault for you in 1960. That was a very generous gift back then; it had the purchasing power of $860 in today's dollars. Looked at in the other direction, however, $100 in 1960 has the purchasing power of $12 today. If your investments don't keep up with inflation, they will lose value every year.

Management Risk. Also called company risk, this encompasses a wide array of factors that can impact the value of a specific company. For example, the managers who run the company might make a bad decision or get embroiled in a scandal, causing a drop in the value of the company's stocks or bonds. There is also the possibility that a key competitor might release a better product or service.

The poster child for management risk is Enron, which *Fortune* magazine named America's most innovative company for six consecutive years. Unfortunately, one of its primary innovations was fraud. An accounting fraud company brought the company to bankruptcy in 2001, and investors lost everything.

Geopolitical Risk. This involves the impact on the market in response to political and social events such as a terrorist attack, war, pandemic, or elections. Such events, whether actual or anticipated, affect investor attitudes toward the market in general, resulting in system-wide fluctuations in asset prices. Consider Greece, whose Gross Domestic Product totaled $201 billion in in 2017, according to the International Monetary Fund. (The U.S. weighed in at $19.4 trillion). Yet Greece's debt problems set world's stock markets on edge in 2010 as investors worried that the effects of a Greek default—or its exit from the Eurozone—would ripple throughout the financial world.

We can increase risks by using the wrong investment strategies at the wrong time. For example, many investment advisors recommend buy-and-hold strategies without consideration of the current market environment. Buying and holding is much riskier—and much harder to do—when the market is at or near a peak. As a result, most investors are not properly prepared when the market declines, and as markets fall, investors show a strong desire to get back to even. That's usually a bad move. Remember, a 50 percent loss requires a 100 percent gain just to return to even.

Others who have missed the majority of a bull market jump in late, often at the worst possible time. This type of investor demonstrates highly risk-averse actions when facing a profit—and more risk-tolerant or risk-seeking behavior when facing a loss. They continue to hold the investment, hoping the price will rise again. This is, of course, the exact opposite of how they should behave.[12]

Similarly, even investors who are supposed to be the savviest tend to overinvest at the top of markets and underinvest at the bottom, when stocks are cheap. For example, corporate insiders—those who buy shares of their own stock legally—were big buyers in 2007. In 2009? Crickets. The same holds true for corporations that buy back their own stocks. They tend to be rotten judges of the value of their own companies.

The challenge of investing is made more complex by our own emotions about the tradeoff between risk and reward. One way that our brains resolve this conflict is to seek safety in numbers; in other words, to reassure ourselves that we're with the rest of the investment crowd. Safety in numbers is the hypothesis that suggests that by being part of a large physical group or mass, an individual is less likely to be the victim of a mishap, accident, attack, or other bad event.

William Donald Hamilton, widely recognized as one of the most significant evolutionary theorists of the twentieth century, proposed the "selfish herd theory" in 1971 to explain why animals seek central positions in groups. Individuals can reduce their own risk of danger by situating themselves with neighbors all around, so they move toward the center of the group.[13] The effect was tested on a brown fur seal population that was hunted by great white sharks. Using decoys, the distance between the imitation

---

[12] Kahneman, Daniel and Amos Tversky. "Prospect Theory: An Analysis of Decision Under Risk." *Econometrica*, vol. 47, no. 2, 1979, pp. 263-29. https://www.jstor.org/stable/1914185. Accessed 12 October 2018.

[13] Hamilton, W. "Geometry for the Selfish Herd." *Journal of Theoretical Biology*, vol. 31, no. 2, 1971, pp. 295-311. https://doi.org/10.1016/0022-5193 (71)90189-5. Accessed 12 October 2018.

seals and the sharks was varied to produce different domains of danger. Some of the fake seals were situated on the perimeter of the population, while others were placed in the center of the group. The seals on the outskirts of the group, with a greater domain of danger had, as predicted, an increased risk of shark attack. So how does the selfish herd theory apply to investor behavior? Large stock market trends often begin and end with periods of frenzied buying or selling. Many observers cite these episodes as clear examples of herding behavior that is irrational and driven by emotion, when individual investors join the crowd of others as they rush to get in or out of the market.[14]

The typical non-professional investor is putting hard-earned money in the market, hoping for a gain, but wanting to protect the money against losses. However, they often get their information without considering the biases and foibles of their sources: friends, family, and co-workers. Even news from the financial press cannot necessarily be trusted. The financial media uses your fear during market declines and your excitement during markets rebounds to affect your behavior and encourage a reaction to buy or sell. Wall Street and media pundits view investors as a source of liquidity; individuals can be counted on to buy when the big traders are selling (at the top), and vice versa. Furthermore, Wall Street is driven by fees. The more they can get people lathered up to move money around, the better for their revenue. Money in motion creates fees and commissions. And your Uncle Fred is, shall we say, a big talker who will tell you stories about how he made big bucks in the market, and encourage you to jump in during a raging bull market. (He'll rarely talk about his big losses.)

While you cannot completely avoid market declines or cycles, you can apply the disciplined and measured approach of the Adaptive Investment Portfolio to minimize or even benefit from them.

---

[14] Brunnermeirer, Markus K. *Asset Pricing under Asymmetric Information: Bubbles, Crashes, Technical Analysis, and Herding*, Oxford University Press, 2001.

CHAPTER 3

ACTIVE VS. PASSIVE INVESTMENT MANAGEMENT

If you know the enemy and know yourself you need not fear the results of a hundred battles.
- Sun Tzu

History is filled with great struggles: Sparta vs. Athens, Rome vs. Carthage, and active managers vs. passive ones. Most advisors will take sides. But with the Adaptive Investment Portfolio, you'll apply both, because both have their uses.

While the debate between active managers and passive managers might not inspire epic poetry, it is one of the most hotly-debated topics in finance, with billions of dollars riding on the outcome. In 2017, $181 billion fled actively-managed mutual funds and exchange-traded funds, while passively-managed funds and ETFs welcomed $199.6 billion, according to Morningstar Direct.

On one side of the debate there is the active camp, who believe that a canny manager can spot stocks that are set to soar and beat the market averages. On the other? The passive camp, who think that it's impossible to beat the indices for any extended period of time, and that studying all the different strategies for picking stocks is about as worthwhile as searching for Atlantis.

PASSIVE MANAGEMENT

Let's hear from the passive side first. Passive investing holds that markets are efficient and extremely difficult to beat, especially after costs. Thousands of analysts and investors examine stocks like Amazon and Procter & Gamble every day. The odds that one person will figure out something that everyone else has missed is unlikely, to say the least. Furthermore, frequent trading and management fees add costs to the active investment process. It's hard enough to beat the Standard & Poor's 500 stock index without losing 1.5 percent in fees every year.

So passive investors figure that it's smarter to simply track an index, such as the S&P, rather than try to beat it. The result—the index fund. If the fund keeps its expenses low, it's likely to do better than the average comparable actively-managed fund over time. For instance, at the end of 1975, John Bogle launched the First Index Investment Trust, later renamed the Vanguard 500, which was the first stock index fund for individual investors. Now one of the largest mutual funds in the world, the Vanguard 500 Index fund manages more than $417 billion, and is a good example of how the mutual fund industry has eagerly adopted passive methodologies. Its investor shares charge just 0.14 percent a year, or $14 per $10,000 invested. According to Morningstar's system of fund classification, the Vanguard 500 Index fund is a large-company blend fund. Over the past fifteen years, it has beaten 71 percent of all large-company blend funds.

The idea of passively-managed funds started to really attract attention as early as 1952. That is when a student of linear programming, Harry Markowitz, first introduced the world of finance to his paper entitled "Portfolio Selection." In it Markowitz establishes his theory linking risk and return. Markowitz defines risk as variance.

How far the returns vary is defined and quantified by how far the returns could vary from an investment's expected average, or mean, return. A fund that can vary 14 percentage points above or below its average return is riskier than one that varies seven points above or below its average return. The mean-variance approach became the foundation of risk management.

Mean Variance was used as a proxy for risk because assets whose prices were more volatile were seen as more likely to produce losses. A portfolio that gives maximum return for a given risk, or minimum risk for a given return, is an efficient portfolio. Hence, portfolios are selected as follows.

1. From the portfolios that have the same return, the investor will prefer the portfolio with lower risk;
and
2. From the portfolios that have the same risk level, an investor will prefer the portfolio with a higher rate of return.

It was the first time anyone had formally quantified the trade of between risk and return. A rational investor would like to have a higher return. A risk-averse investor would want to have lower risk. With a focus on how an asset's returns correlated with other assets, mathematicians were able to create groups of portfolios which minimized risk for a given level of return, or that maximized return for a given level of risk. These large portfolios formulate what Markowitz termed the "efficient frontier," and that helped inspire today's highly-diversified, passively managed funds.

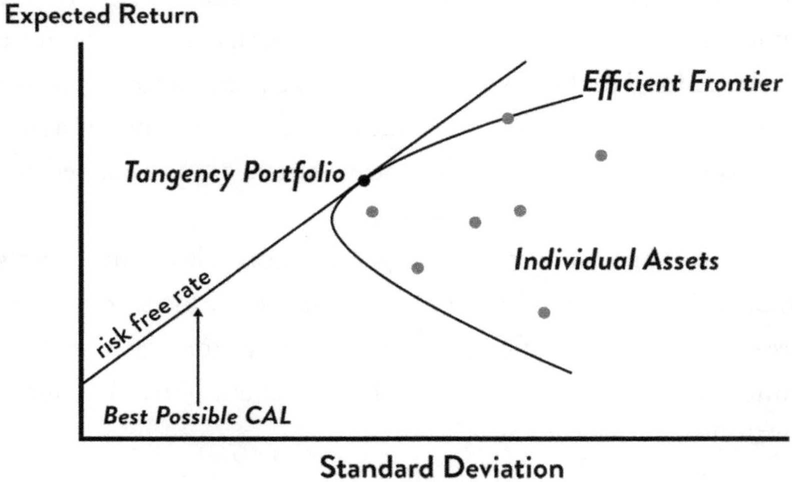

Figure 4.[15] The hyperbola is sometimes referred to as the 'Markowitz Bullet', and its upward sloped portion is the efficient frontier if no risk-free asset is available. With a risk-free asset, the straight line is the efficient frontier.

Passive investing also relies on Modern Portfolio Theory, which is comprised of four basic concepts.

1. Investors tend to dislike risk, and given two portfolios with the same return, they will choose the one with the least risk.
2. Over time, riskier assets provide higher expected returns as compensation to investors for accepting greater risk.
3. Adding high risk, low-correlation asset classes to a portfolio can actually reduce volatility and increase expected rates of return. (Correlation refers to a technique used to measure the relationship between two or asset classes. A correlation of 1.0, means that the two tend to move in perfect tandem with

[15] "Efficient Frontier." *Wikipedia*. 13 June 2018. https://en.wikipedia.org/wiki/Efficient_frontier. Accessed 12 October 2018.

No Clear Winner in Active vs. Passive Large-Cap Funds

Winners	Active Large Blend Category (%)	S&P 500 Index Funds (%)
1985	29.46	**31.34**
1986	**17.74**	17.28
1987	2.92	**4.08**
1988	**16.09**	15.47
1989	27.46	**30.45**
1990	-3.37	**-3.35**
1991	**33.35**	29.50
1992	**9.63**	7.05
1993	**12.40**	9.46
1994	-0.74	**0.86**
1995	33.14	**36.87**
1996	22.29	**22.48**
1997	29.88	**32.71**
1998	20.49	**28.20**
1999	19.25	**20.31**
2000	**-0.26**	-9.45
2001	**-8.54**	-12.35
2002	**-20.15**	-22.46
2003	**28.85**	27.93
2004	**10.98**	10.32
2005	**6.82**	4.41
2006	14.52	**15.19**
2007	**7.03**	4.97
2008	**-36.92**	-37.26
2009	**28.88**	25.98
2010	14.09	**14.50**
2011	-0.60	**1.62**
2012	15.29	**15.41**
2013	**32.20**	31.71
2014	11.13	**13.08**
2015	-0.98	**0.89**
2016	10.21	**11.42**
2017	20.05	**21.26**

Source: Morningstar, 1/18

Figure 5.[16]

[16] "The cyclical nature of active & passive investing." *Hartford Funds*. First quarter 2018. https://www.hartfordfunds.com/dam/en/docs/pub/whitepapers/WP287.pdf. Accessed 24 October 2018.

each other. A correlation of zero means that the relationship between them is completely random. A negative correlation means that they tend to move in exactly the opposite direction).

4. Passive asset class fund portfolios can be designed with the expectations of delivering the highest expected returns over time for a chosen level of risk.

These concepts, however, assume that all risk can be measured, which is a somewhat dubious assumption. In the early 1930s John Maynard Keynes[17] indicated that some of the risk in the stock market could not be quantified and measured. Keynes, who advocated the use of fiscal and monetary policy to stimulate the economy during recessions, was also an extremely successful investor, rolling up a £500,000 fortune (in 1946 currency) by the time of his death.

Keynes believed that the theory of diversification is flawed, stating, "To suppose that safety...consists in having a small gamble in a large number of different [stocks] where I have no information... as compared with a substantial stake in a company where one's information is adequate, strikes me as a travesty of investment policy."[18]

William F. Sharpe later picked up Markowitz's ideas to create the backbone of the Capital Asset Pricing Model (CAPM), which helped to make Markowitz's work more user-friendly. Sharpe, who won the Nobel Prize in Economics in 1990, introduced the "beta"

[17] John Maynard Keynes (June 5, 1883-April 21st, 1946) was a British economist whose ideas fundamentally changed the theory and practice of economic policies in government. His ideas are the basis for the school of thought known as Keynesian economics.

[18] John Maynard Keynes, Letter to F.C Scott, February 6, 1942.

coefficient.[19] A stock with a beta of 1.25, for example, would rise or fall 1.25 percent as much as the S&P 500, while one with a beta of .80 would rise or fall 0.80 percent as much as the index.

The idea according to CAPM was to diversify away stock-specific risk, leaving only market (systemic) risk, which is defined by beta. According to the theory, investors would be unwise to hold a small number of stocks because they are taking stock-specific risk when they do not have to.

Although deeply rooted in Modern Portfolio Theory (MPT), the passive approach also draws heavily on the Efficient-Market Hypothesis developed in the 1970s by Nobel Prize laureate Eugene Fama, considered the father of the Efficient Market Hypothesis.

The Efficient Market Hypothesis (EMH) is a theory in financial economics which states that all stocks are perfectly priced and fully reflect all available information and therefore, Fama argued, stocks always trade at fair value. Consider Microsoft stock, for example. Legions of analysts examine the company's financial statements, products, and management every day. Could one analyst spot something no one else has? It's possible—but even if so, any advantage the analyst had wouldn't last long before others discovered the same thing.

If so, it is impossible for investors to purchase undervalued stocks or sell stocks for inflated prices, making it impossible to outperform the overall market through expert stock selections or market timing. According to the EMH, the only way an investor can possibly obtain higher returns is by chance or by purchasing

---

[19] ...which helped to standardize the process of evaluating assets and their risk premium by incorporating a security's variance versus an underlying index (rather than versus every other security in a portfolio) and that represented systemic risk.

riskier investments.[20]

The Efficient Market Hypothesis is commonly presented in three forms:

1. Weak-form efficiency: future prices cannot be predicted by analyzing past prices or past returns.
2. Semi-strong-form efficiency: in addition to point 1, share prices adjust to publicly-available new information very quickly and in an unbiased fashion, such that no excess returns can be earned by trading on that information.
3. Strong-form efficiency: in addition to point 2, share prices reflect all information, public and private, and no one can earn excess returns.

Mean Variance, the Capital Asset Pricing Model, and the Efficient Market Hypothesis, are classified together as Modern Portfolio Theory and are the bedrock for much of modern financial economics and the passive investment approach.

Consistent with the EMH is the Random Walk Hypothesis, stating that price changes are, at least to observers, random and unpredictable—a random walk—so prices are random and therefore cannot be predicted. This concept can be traced back to a French broker, Jules Regnault, who published a book about it in 1863, and then to French mathematician Louis Bachelier, whose doctoral dissertation of 1900 was entitled "The Theory of Speculation."

More recently, Burton G. Malkiel, an economics professor at Princeton University and author of *A Random Walk Down Wall Street*, performed a test where his students were given a hypothetical stock that was initially worth $50. The closing stock price each

---

[20] Van Bergen, Jason. "Efficient Market Hypothesis: Is The Stock Market Efficient?" 17 February 2004. *Investopedia*. 7 February 2004. https://www.investopedia.com/articles/basics/04/022004.asp. Accessed 12 October, 2018.

day was determined by a coin flip. If the result was heads, the price would close a half point higher, but if the result was tails, it would close a half point lower. Each time, the price had a 50-50 chance of closing higher or lower than the previous day. Malkiel then took the results in the form of a graph to a chart technician to analyze the patterns.[21] The technician told Malkiel that he needed to buy the stock immediately. Malkiel argued that this indicated that the market and stocks could be just as random as flipping a coin. The suggestion here is that since the chart was a result of a random coin flips, there was no actual trend, the chartist recommendation was based on random data via the coin flip, thus not an adequate method of analysis.

Some have argued that the stock market is "micro-efficient" but not "macro-efficient," meaning that the EMH is much better suited for individual stocks than it is for the aggregate stock market.[22] Andrew W. Lo and Archie Craig MacKinlay, professors of finance at the MIT Sloan School of Management and the University of Pennsylvania respectively, have presented evidence that they believe shows the Random Walk Hypothesis to be wrong. Their book, *A Non-Random Walk Down Wall Street*, presents a number of tests and studies that support the view that there are trends in the stock market and that the stock market is somewhat predictable.[23]

In rebuttal to the EMH, Andrew Lo has proposed the Adaptive

---

[21] Keane, Simon M. *Stock Market Efficiency*. Philip Allan Limited, 1983.

[22] Jung, Jeeman and Robert Shiller. "Samuelson's Dictum And The Stock Market." *Economic Inquiry*, vol 43, no. 2, 2005, pp. 221-228. http://www.econ.yale.edu//~shiller/pubs/p1183.pdf. Accessed 13 October 2018.

[23] Lo, Andrew W. and A. Craig Mackinlay, *A Non-Random Walk Down Wall Street* (5th ed.), Princeton University Press, 2002.

Market Hypothesis[24], an attempt to reconcile economic theories based on the Efficient Market Hypothesis with behavioral economics by applying the principles of evolution to financial interactions: competition, adaptation, and natural selections.[25] According to Lo, market efficiency cannot be evaluated without considering additional factors. Much of "irrational" investor behavior—loss aversion, overconfidence, and overreaction—are, in fact, consistent with the evolutionary model of individuals adapting to changing environment. Cave men who didn't have a good sense of the fight or flight instinct, for example, didn't leave descendants. And investors who don't have a well-honed sense of when to buy and when to sell may leave descendants but not leave any inheritance for them to live on.

The Adaptive Market Hypothesis has several characteristics that differentiate it from the Efficient Market Hypothesis. For example, Lo argues that the degree of market efficiency depends on factors in the market environment, such as the number of competitors, the magnitude of profit opportunities available, and the adaptability of the market participants. Lo suggests that the best way of achieving a constant level of expected returns is to adapt to changing market conditions.

Most recently, there has been a lot of focus and a sense of triumph on the continued rise of passive investing, which has enjoyed strong performance since the financial crises of 2008. However, just because one style of investing has come into favor

---

[24] Lo, Andrew. "The Adaptive Market Hypothesis: Market Efficiency from an Evolutionary Perspective." *Journal of Portfolio Management*, vol. 5, no. 30, 2004, pp. 15-29. http://web.mit.edu/alo/www/main.html. Accessed 12 October 2018.

[25] Lo, Andrew (2005) "Reconciling Efficient Markets with Behavioral Finance: The Adaptive Markets Hypothesis." *Journal of Investment Consulting*, vol. 7, no. 2, 2005, pp. 21-44. http://alo.mit.edu/wp-content/uploads/2015/06/ReconcilingEffMarkets2005.pdf. Accessed 12 October 2018.

does not mean others are going the way of the dodo. It is important to remember that experienced managers or strategists who underperform during any period are likely to outperform in the following period, and the previously outperforming managers are likely to underperform. This is due the nature of market cycles and is exactly why diversification is such an important part of portfolio construction.

As an example, consider the rocky start in 2018 for global equity markets as volatility had returned with a bang. February saw the first 10 percent market correction in a long time. Interestingly, while the volatility experienced at that time is a very normal part of dynamic markets, investors have been so conditioned to the steady rise in equity prices that the upheaval has almost immediately activated some the behavioral traits and personal biases such as loss aversion and recency bias—the belief that recently-observed patterns will continue into the future. On the contrary, it seems reasonable that yesterday's events should not necessarily determine how tomorrow's investment decisions are made.

ACTIVE MANAGEMENT

On the other side of the active vs. passive debate are those who believe that good managers can beat the index. The current hero of active management is Will Danoff, manager of the Fidelity Contrafund. In the fifteen year-period which ended in June 2018, Danoff has driven the fund to an 11.89 percent average annual gain vs. 9.3 percent for the S&P 500 with dividends reinvested. The all-time champion, of course, is Warren Buffett, CEO of Berkshire Hathaway.

Buffett, a native of Omaha, Nebraska, was an acolyte of Benjamin Graham, the co-author of Security Analysis, the Bible of value investors. In 1964, Buffett and his business partner, Charlie Munger, bought textile manufacturer Berkshire Hathaway and transformed it into a diversified holding company. The company stock has gained 20.9 percent annually through 2017 vs. 9.9 percent for the S&P 500. A $10,000 investment in Berkshire Hathaway in 1964 would have been worth more than $240 million at the end of 2017.[26]

Active investment management is a strategy where the portfolio manager makes specific investments with the objective of outperforming a benchmark index, such as the S&P 500. The idea is to exploit market inefficiencies and purchase stocks that are undervalued, or to sell short those that are overvalued. Active strategies seek to uncover value and defend gains in a market where little is cheap. An active manager can choose a variety of specific stocks, sectors, or industries instead of investing in a broadly-diversified index fund that would be more common for a passive manager.

Active strategies can offer tremendous flexibility to address an investor's individual needs. They can manage risk by hedging or simply avoiding areas that look unprofitable. They can also manage the tax burden on a portfolio. (To be fair, most index funds are highly tax efficient.) The value of active strategies' ability to act differently than an index or index fund is never clearer than when markets become volatile. While passive strategies capture all of an index's gains, it also participates in all of the losses when times are tough. Active strategies can proactively shift positions or go to all cash during market declines in order to seek shelter, with the goal of capital preservation.

[26] Frankel, Matthew, CFP. "Here's How Much $10,000 Invested in Berkshire Hathaway Stock in 1964 is Worth Now." *The Motley Fool.* 24 July, 2017. https://www.fool.com/investing/2017/07/24/heres-how-much-10000-invested-in-berkshire-hathawa.aspx. Accessed 12 October 2018.

Right on cue, as a result of the market volatility that began in late January 2018, active managers starting receiving a lot more attention. Active management has typically outperformed passive management during market corrections, because some good active managers can capture alpha[27] as the market recovers. In fact, from 2000 to 2009, active management outperformed passive nine out of ten years.[28] To demonstrate, look at Morningstar Large Blend, which is the largest Morningstar category, with $2.43 trillion in net assets, comprising 16 percent of the U.S. mutual fund market.[29] This category is interesting to study because it is widely considered to be the most efficient, which is the precise market condition where active investing supposedly makes the least amount of sense. To represent active management only, all index funds and enhanced index funds have been removed. The Morningstar S&P 500 tracking category has been used for passive management strategies.

The passive large-blend strategies *did* outperform active large-blend strategies in four of the last five years, which helps to explain why in 2017 passive U.S. equity funds had inflows of $224 billion, while more than $197 billion under active management was redeemed.[30] But the past five years do not tell the whole

[27] The measure of the performance of a portfolio after adjusting for risk. Alpha is calculated by comparing the volatility of the portfolio and comparing it to some benchmark. The alpha is the excess return of the portfolio over the benchmark.

[28] Source: Hartford Funds. Data source: Morningstar, 1/18. *Active Large Blend is made up of funds from the Morningstar Large Blend category that are not index or enhanced index funds. *S&P 500 Index Funds are represented by the Morningstar S&P 500 tracking category.

[29] Source: Morningstar Direct, 1/18. *Active Large Blend is made up of funds from the Morningstar Large Blend category that are not index or enhanced index funds. *S&P 500 Index Funds are represented by the Morningstar S&P 500 tracking category.

* All investments are subject to risks, including the possible loss of principal. Performance data quoted represents past performance and does not guarantee future results.

[30] Source: Morningstar Direct, 1/18.

story. A broader look at the chart shows active and passive have traded the lead in performance over time like two evenly-matched boxers competing in a big prize fight. From 2000 to 2009, active outperformed passive nine years out of ten. During the ten years before that, passive outperformed active seven years out of ten.

Over the last thirty two years, active has outperformed 15 times, while passive outperformed 17 times. While the cyclical nature of the performance attributes apply to the Morningstar Large Blend Category, it also applies to other investment categories such as mid-cap, small cap, and global equities. What this demonstrates is that while it may be difficult to decide whether active or passive is the overall winner over the past thirty years, you can determine a clear winner in active vs. passive performance over certain designated cycles. The recent outperformance of passive, which was preceded by a ten-year period of active outperformance, may soon trade the lead again.

Warren Buffett is probably the most eloquent spokesman for active management. Here's an excerpt of what he said in a 1984 speech at the Columbia Business School, where he stated that nine investors independently investing in different companies achieved far superior returns than did index funds:

> So these are nine records of "coin flippers" from Graham-and-Doddsville. I haven't selected them with hindsight from among thousands. It's not like I am reciting to you the names of a bunch of lottery winners—people I have never heard of before they won the lottery. I selected these men years ago based upon their framework for investment decision-making. I know what they had been taught and additionally I had some personal knowledge of their intellect, character, and temperament. It's very important to understand

> that this group has assumed far less risk than average; note their record in years when the general market was weak. While they differ greatly in style, these investors are, mentally, always buying the business, not buying the stock. A few of them sometimes buy whole businesses. Far more often, they simply buy small pieces of businesses. Their attitude, whether buying all or a tiny piece of a business, is the same. Some of them hold portfolios with dozens of stocks; others concentrate on a handful. But all exploit the difference between the market price of a business and its intrinsic value.
>
> I'm convinced that there is much inefficiency in the market. These Graham-and-Doddsville investors have successfully exploited gaps between price and value. When the price of a stock can be influenced by a "herd" on Wall Street with prices set at the margin by the most emotional person, or the greediest person, or the most depressed person, it is hard to argue that the market always prices rationally. In fact, market prices are frequently nonsensical.

One of the greatest names in economics, Robert Shiller[31], has questioned the value and role that passive investing is playing in the bull market. Shiller has compared passive investing to seeing a green light at an intersection and crossing the street without looking both ways. In 2005, just prior to the housing crash, Shiller described the rapid rise of housing prices as a bubble and warned that prices could fall by as much as 40 percent. After the housing bubble did in fact burst, resulting in the market crash and Great Recession, many people argued that it was primarily caused by

---

[31] Robert James Shiller is an American economist (Nobel Laureate, 2013), academic and best-selling author.

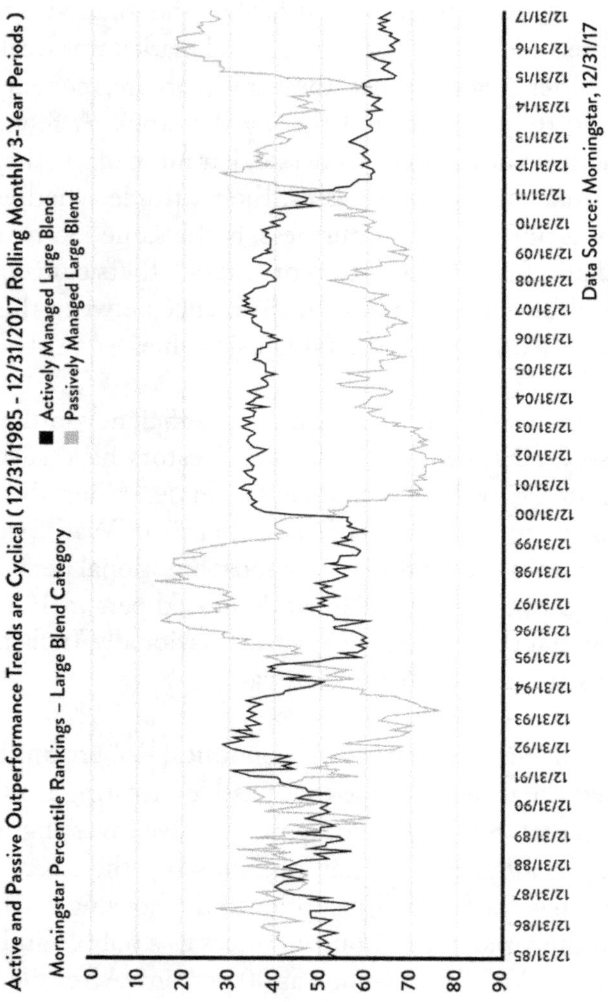

Figure 6.[32]

[32] "The cyclical nature of active & passive investing." *Hartford Funds*. First quarter 2018. https://www.hartfordfunds.com/dam/en/docs/pub/whitepapers/WP287.pdf. Accessed 24 October 2018.

inefficiencies in the credit markets.

In turn, when asked about the real estate "bubble" and credit market inefficiencies, Eugene Fama, who asserts that financial markets are "informationally efficient" said, "I don't even know what that means. People who get credit have to get it from somewhere. Does a credit bubble mean that people save too much during that period? I don't know what a credit bubble means. I don't even know what a bubble means. These words have become popular. I don't think they have any meaning."

So, no matter what the facts are, Fama has his story and he is sticking to it. I will tell you something, there are times when you want to be out of the market—and when the market crashed after the housing bubble burst was one of those times. You can either be adaptive to the market dynamics or be a victim.

Fama and Shiller are two economists who have been on opposing sides in regard to views on the rationality of financial markets. While Fama's work has inspired the rise of passive investing and the index fund, Shiller has been perhaps the most influential critic, and has presented meaningful evidence on irrational, inefficient market behavior that gained notoriety by predicting the fall of stock prices in 2000 as well as the housing crash that began in 2006.

What is fascinating is that despite their differing views, in 2013 Fama and Shiller were jointly awarded the Nobel Memorial Prize in Economic Science, along with a third economist, Lars Peter Hansen, whose work in statistical analysis is used to evaluate theories about price movements. The award described the work as collectively illuminating the workings of financial markets by showing that stock and bond prices move unpredictably in the short term, but with greater predictability over longer periods. The Nobel Prize committee said these findings showed that markets were moved by a mix of rational calculus and irrational behavior.

This theoretical battle is the economic equivalent of Superman vs. Spider-Man, with each economist defending his position and throwing powerful blows. When asked about sharing the prize with Fama, Shiller said the mismatch between Fama's findings and theories must make him feel like a priest who has discovered God does not exist. Shiller and Fama are both economic heroes of mine. Their work in financial markets and economics has helped us all better understand how markets work and how to best construct portfolios. Having said that, I do not believe that in 2018/2019, we should be taking the view that timing doesn't work. Shiller clearly showed that it does.

While most investment professionals come down on one side or the other of the passive vs. active management debate, I feel it is incomplete without additional examination.

In their landmark paper, "Determinants of Portfolio Performance,"[33] Gary P. Brinson, L. Randolph Hood, and Gilbert L. Beebower (BHB) concluded that a portfolio's static asset allocation was the primary determinant of a portfolio's return variability, with security selections and market-timing playing minor roles. This allocation explained most of the total return and volatility over time, providing over 90 percent of a portfolio's return variability.

In the time since the paper was published, several authors have revisited the BHB study, with updates and challenges. While some research has confirmed the study's conclusions, others have criticized it and its adoption by the investment industry. Investment advisors have generally interpreted this research to mean that selecting an appropriate asset allocation is more important than

[33] Brinson, Gary P., L Randolph Hood, and Gilbert L. Beebower. "Determinants of Portfolio Performance." *Financial Analysts Journal*, vol. 42, no 4, 1986. pp. 39-48. [Reprinted in: *Financial Analysts Journal* vol. 51, no. 1, 1995, pp. 133-8 (50th Anniversary Issue.)] https://doi.org/10.2469/faj.v51.n1.1869. Accessed 12 October 2018.

selecting the funds used to implement the allocation.

It seems that some investment advisors found it to be an easy and convenient way to justify not doing the heavy lifting and hard work of investment management. In 1997 William Jahnke published a critique of the BHB study, in which he argued, "The fundamental problem with BHB's analysis is its focus on explaining return volatility rather than portfolio returns. In fact, investors should be more concerned with the range of likely outcomes over their investment planning horizon than the volatility of returns." Further, Jahnke warned, "Fixed asset allocation solutions are inferior to analytically linking forward-looking strategic asset allocation solutions....as the investor's circumstances or market opportunities change, so also should the investor's asset allocation." In his critique, Jahnke referred to the financial industry's misrepresentation and exploitation of the BHB study. In his view, the industries embrace of the study was a failure of responsibility and duty of their active management responsibilities.

In a follow-up study in 2000 by Ibbotson and Kaplan, "Does Asset Allocation Policy Explain 40, 90 or 100 percent of Performance?"[34], Ibbotson and Kaplan concluded that asset allocation did in fact account for over 90 percent of the period-to-period variable returns of a portfolio, but that the total returns were dominated by exposure to the capital markets in general, "a case of a rising tide lifting all boats." Their study concluded that only about 40 percent of the return variation between the funds studied was due to asset allocation, with the remainder of returns due to other factors, including asset-timing, style within asset classes, security selection, and fees.

[34] Ibbotson, Roger G. and Paul D. Kaplan. "Does Asset Allocation Policy Explain 40, 90, or 100 Percent of Performance?" *Financial Analysts Journal*, vol. 56, no. 1, 2000, pp. 26-33. https://doi.org/10.2469/faj.v56.n1.2327. Accessed 12 October 2018.

In 2010, Roger Ibbotson and Associates presented a paper entitled, "The Equal Importance of Asset Allocation and Active Management."[35] They addressed the heavily-debated question of the relative importance of asset allocation policy versus active portfolio management in explaining variability in performance. They concluded that asset allocation and active management are equally important in determining portfolio return differences, and that cyclical market movements were the primary driver of investment returns. They studied ten years of returns for more than 5,000 mutual funds in order to measure the relative importance of asset allocation policy versus active portfolio management. In the paper, they noted that the BHB study did not separate the market returns from the incremental impact of asset allocation policy. Ibbotson later commented on their findings, saying, "About three-quarters of a typical funds variation in time-series returns comes from general market movement, with the remaining portion split about evenly between the specific asset allocation and active management."

While the rivalry between active management vs. passive management has evolved into a progressively complex and circular argument, where does all of this leave you, the investor? In a market that has become increasingly homogenized by massive, overly-diversified super funds, there now exists an exciting opportunity for the informed investor that is fundamentally focused and adaptive.

Historically, going back to the 1900s, investors in U.S. stocks have been able to realize real capital gains of about 7 percent per year. No other asset class—bonds, cash, gold or real estate—has offered comparable return potential over time. Having said that,

---

[35] Xiong, James X. CFA, Roger G. Ibbotson, Thomas M. Idzorek, CFA, and Peng Chen, CFA. "The Equal Importance of Asset Allocation and Active Management." *Financial Analysts Journal*, vol. 66, no. 4, 2010, pp. 16-17. https://doi.org/10.2469/faj.v66.n4.12. Accessed 12 October 2018.

stock markets are subject to periods of wild volatility and the expected returns largely depend on time in the market. For example, during any given one-year period, your returns are much more variable than in any given twenty-year period.

And that's one of the potential problems with passive investing for the long term. As we discussed in the previous chapter, few people have the stomach to withstand the stock market's short-term gyrations. Despite an investor's best intentions to buy and hold over the long term, the reality is that the vast majority of investors don't do that. Once we have processed the important aspects of our own behavioral biases, how we make decisions, our attitudes about risk, and the difference between passive management and active management, we are prepared to study the next step on our way to the Adaptive Investment Portfolio: the economy.

CHAPTER 4

UNDERSTANDING THE ECONOMY

Anyone who believes that exponential growth can go on forever in a finite world is either a madman or an economist.
- Kenneth Boulding

Some things in life are simply beyond your control. Sure, you expect the sun to shine on your parade and get upset when the weather doesn't comply with your wishes. You expect everything to go according to plan and get stressed out when it doesn't turn out that way. Some folks feel they are entitled to guarantees. (Good luck with that.) Can a wish banish clouds from the sky? No, not in real life. So it may be time to end your wishful thinking about controlling the uncontrollable and learn to adapt to complex situations. On the day of the big parade, a prudent person would carry an umbrella if it looks like rain, and simply reschedule the parade altogether if they expect a storm that is more severe. Better to go catch a movie on that day and wait for the sun to come out. In investing, as in life, you should expect the unexpected. Keeping an eye on the economy, the markets, and the Federal Reserve can help you avoid major storms—which is one reason why the Adaptive Investment Portfolio is, well, adaptive. Different market climates call for different strategies.

ECONOMICS

Many see economics as a very dry subject filled with diagrams and statistics. It is. That's why economics is called the dismal science by some. Nevertheless, economics doesn't have to be dull. Just like the most riveting novel, it involves human beings and the vagaries of their individual choices and behaviors, running the gamut of money, markets, borrowing, consumption, and trade instead of sex, romance, or intrigue.

Economics deals with individual choice and behavior. Macroeconomics focuses on the big picture: employment, production, inflation, and monetary and fiscal policy. Microeconomics is the study and analysis of the behavior of firms and individuals, and how things like prices and markets work.

But not even the experts always agree. An old joke says that if you were to line up all the world's economists from end to end, they wouldn't reach agreement. Those disagreements started with one of the earliest books on economics, Adam Smith's *An Inquiry into the Nature and Causes of The Wealth of Nations*, published in 1776. Smith argued that narrow self-interest could order economic activity. "It is not from the benevolence of the butcher, the brewer, or the baker that we expect our dinner, but from their regard to their own interest. We address ourselves, not to their humanity but to their self-love, and never talk to them of our own necessities but of their advantages.[36]"

Even Smith acknowledged that narrow self-interest was not always for the best, as it was difficult to regulate businesses from this perspective.

---

[36] Smith, Adam. *An Inquiry into the Nature and Causes of the Wealth of Nations: Book 1 Chapter 2.* 1776. https://www.econlib.org/library/Smith/smWN.html. Accessed 12 October 2018.

"People of the same trade seldom meet together, even for merriment and diversion, but the conversation ends in a conspiracy against the public, or in some contrivance to raise prices," Smith wrote. "It is impossible indeed to prevent such meetings, by any law which either could be executed, or would be consistent with liberty or justice. But though the law cannot hinder people of the same trade from sometimes assembling together, it ought to do nothing to facilitate such assemblies; much less to render them necessary."[37]

Current economists agree that spending is what drives our economy. It accounts for about 70 percent of our GDP, which is the total value of goods produced and services provided in a country during one year. When consumption increases for a particular good or service, production must increase to meet that demand. The increase in consumer demand creates jobs, because production must increase to meet those demands. The increase in employment creates more consumption as those newly-employed have income to spend on goods and services.

Naturally, the reverse is true—when consumer spending decreases, production must decrease, resulting in the elimination of jobs as production slows down. The elimination of jobs means that there are fewer people who have money to spend on goods and services, resulting in an economic slowdown or contraction. This is how free-market capitalism works in an economic and political system that is controlled by private owners for profit and not by the government.

The ebb and flow fluctuation of this economic activity results in a business cycle that is typically comprised of five phases: expansion, peak, recession, trough, and recovery. Extreme periods of expansion

[37] Ibid. p. 152

or contraction are referred to as periods of boom and bust.

The system works very well, but does come with some notable extremes in wealth and poverty.

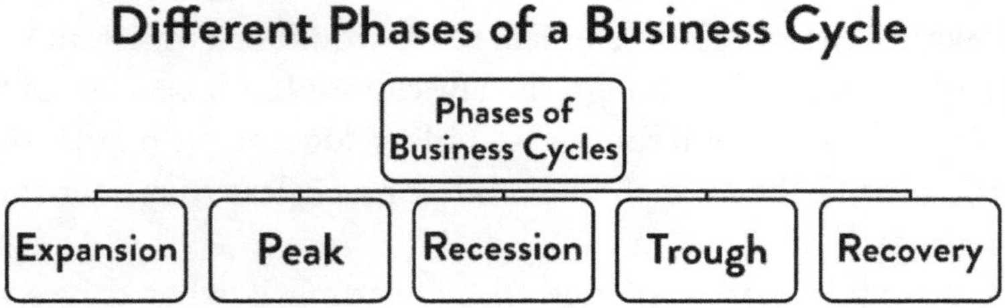

Figure 7.

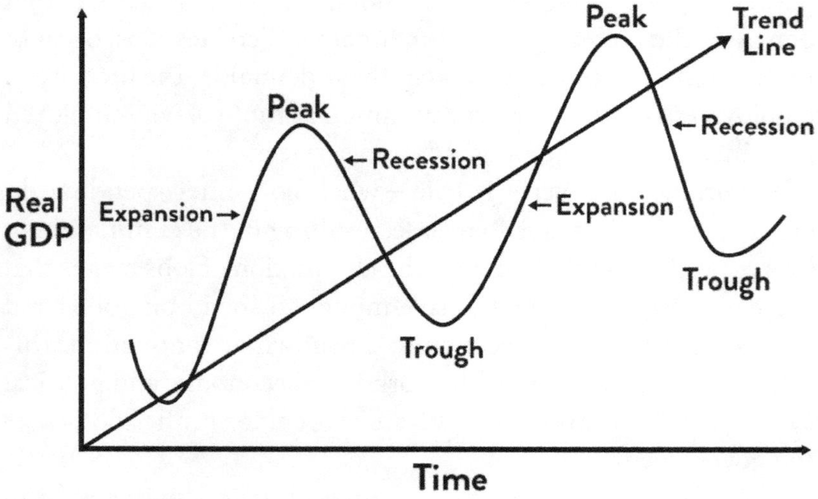

Figure 8.

John Maynard Keynes, developed ideas on how to smooth out the economic and business cycles. The basics of his theory challenged the idea that free markets would automatically provide employment if workers were flexible with their wage demands. Keynes argued that governments could smooth out the volatility of free markets by expanding the supply of money and running large budget deficits during periods of economic slowdown. The answer, he suggested, "is not to be found in abolishing booms and thus keeping us permanently in a semi-slump; but in abolishing slumps and thus keeping us permanently in a quasi-boom."[38]

Politicians love the Keynesian approach, as it offers a seemingly pain-free solution to encourage employment and economic growth without raising taxes. Sweet! Actually, Keynes did believe that the government should raise taxes and interest rates during economic recovery to cool the economy and prevent inflation. Cutting government spending during a recession only deepened the misery and prolonged the downturn, he argued.

Unfortunately, many politicians don't seem to have read Keynes all the way through and prefer the having-their-cake-and-eating-it-too version. They view Keynesianism much like a miracle weight-loss diet that promises an amazing transformation with no dieting or exercise.

The Keynesian view comes into stark contrast with the "Austrian School," a strain of economic thought that suggests that it is, in fact, the banks' issuance of credit that causes economic fluctuations. When banks extend credit at artificially low interest rates, it causes a misallocation of resources called "malinvestment." The Austrians argue that the business cycle is a self-inflicted consequence of excessive growth, and that recessions are necessary in order for markets to make corrections for the decisions made during the

---

[38] Keynes, John Maynard. *The General Theory of Employment, Interest and Money in The Collected Writings of John Maynard Keynes*, Macmillan, London, 1973.

"cheap money" booms that always precede the bust.[39]

Friedrich Hayek, a prominent member of the Austrian School, opposed any interference in markets. Downturns were essential to allow capitalism and markets to purge and renew themselves. Hayek believed that Keynes' general theory of employment, interest, and money was primarily motivated by political and economic problems. Hayek felt that Keynesian economics would not solve the problems but would create inflation. Keynes, of course, was equally critical of Hayek's work, calling it a "farrago of nonsense."

The table below summarizes the main differences between the two schools of economic thought.[40]

AUSTRIAN	KEYNESIAN
Free-Markets	Government Intervention
Sound Money Under a Gold Standard	Fiat Currency
Savings	Debt
Investment	Consumption
Deflation is Good	Deflation is Bad
Let Inefficient Corporations Fail	Bailouts

Figure 9.

---

[39] von Misses, Ludwig. *Theory of Money and Credit*, Part III, Part IV, 1912. https://mises.org/library/theory-money-and-credit. Accessed 12 October 2018.

[40] Ferreira, Chris. "Keynesian vs. Austrian Economics." *Economic Reason.* 30 October 2012. http://www.economicreason.com/austrianeconomics/keynesian-vs-austrian-economics/. Accessed 12 October 2018.

The easiest way to explain the differences between the two schools is with a comparison of how nature deals with the overgrowth of the forest. While forest fires are often harmful and destructive and are a major concern in many parts of the U.S., they are actually an important part of maintaining a natural and healthy ecosystem. It is now well understood that human intervention to prevent naturally-occurring wildfires can actually cause larger, hotter, and faster-moving fires, leading to massive destruction. When nature starts them, wildfires play an integral role in the environment. They return nutrients to the soil by burning dead or decaying matter. They also act as a disinfectant, removing disease-ridden plants and harmful insects from a forest ecosystem. By burning through thick canopies and brushy undergrowth, wildfires allow sunlight to reach the forest floor, enabling a new generation of healthy seedlings to grow.[41]

The comparison of wildfires to economic self-correction mirrors the Austrian view of the relationship between the free market and government intervention. Austrians believe that "nature" should be allowed to run its course, and that the less the government interferes in free markets, the better it is. Like naturally-occurring forest fires, Austrians believe that a recession or depression is the process by which the economy adjusts to the wastes and errors of an economic boom, and reestablishes efficient, healthy, and sustainable conditions. These conditions support new business opportunities and efficient capital allocation.

While Keynesians believe their approach has a bit more sympathy for "woodland creatures," and seeks to limit the worst of naturally-occurring economic cycles. Austrians would argue that the Keynesian approach results in a bigger, hotter, faster and more

---

[41] "Climate: 101. *National Geographic*. https://www.nationalgeographic.com/environment/natural-disasters/wildfires/. Accessed 12 October 2018.

destructive clearing event. As an example, the solution to the 2008 financial crisis was to offer remedies which were essentially more of the same thing that caused the crisis in the first place: cheaper money and more debt. That was in fact also the solution for the Black Monday stock market crash in 1987 and the 2001 dot-com stock market crash. We now live in a world that is swimming in debt, and we have low, but rising interest rates to boot. Debt and interest rates matter. At some point the bill will come due. It will either get paid, or the forest fire will burn all the trees down!

Now, just like ten years ago, as long as the market keeps going up, nobody is actually scared or even cautious. Why should they be? Just like a glass or two of fine wine with dinner, it feels good and everyone is enjoying a good time. However, while we know that more than a drink or two can have unpleasant consequences, it has been a while since we had a hangover and the memory of that bad feeling seems far away. After the third drink or so the music sounds great, you are dancing away, and wouldn't describe yourself as drunk. If the music keeps playing, and the party keeps going, certainly the good times will continue as well, with no worries about any repercussions the next day. People don't want to think about that; they don't want the fun to stop. The hangover hits the next day after the drinking has stopped. Similarly, fear only comes in the markets when the easy money policies and credit expansion party ceases and the selling begins. By then, it's always too late to do anything about the outcome as another bubble bursts.

Prior to the financial crisis in 2008, no Federal Reserve officials had publicly identified any economic problems or concerns. Even as the housing market began to fall apart, Ben Bernanke, the chairman of the Federal Reserve at the time, continued to insist the housing market was stable. He had absolutely no idea the financial crisis was coming.

In one instance he said, "We've never had a decline in housing prices on a nationwide basis. So, what I think is more likely is that house prices will slow, maybe stabilize, might slow consumption spending a bit. I don't think it's gonna drive the economy too far from its full employment path, though."[42] July 2005

Granted it took a couple of years to manifest, but by early 2007 there were clear signs of distress in the credit markets. By that time, lenders began tightening their belts when it came to housing projects. I have a good friend who is a very large multi-family housing (apartments) investor. He would put together a few large apartment buildings of 500 units or so each, where he identified opportunities to create value, raise rents, and hopefully sell the apartment buildings at some point in the future for a profit. He had a strong balance sheet and a good track record and obtaining financing for these properties was routine. In 2007 the multi-family real estate market started to soften dramatically, and he could no longer secure financing for new deals. Large operators like my friend saw the writing on the wall, but the Fed did not.

Market conditions continued to worsen and yet were not acknowledged by the Fed. "At this juncture, however, the impact on the broader economy and financial markets of the problems in the subprime market seems likely to be contained. In particular, mortgages to prime borrowers and fixed-rate mortgages to all classes of borrowers continue to perform well, with low rates of delinquency," says Bernanke.[43]

---

[42] Costa, Gareth. "GFC 10 years on: Fed fiddled as houses burned." *The West Australian.* 26 August 2018. https://thewest.com.au/business/economy/gfc-10-years-on-fed-fiddled-as-houses-burned-ng-b88923113z. Accessed 14 October 2018.

[43] Bernanke, Ben S. "The Economic Outlook." *Board of Governors of the Federal Reserve.* 28 March 2007. https://www.federalreserve.gov/newsevents/testimony/bernanke20070328a.htm. Accessed 14 October 2008.

We ended up having what is now referred to as the "Great Recession," the worst economic crisis since the Great Depression. So you are not going to get a "heads up" from the Fed on the next market crises. The financial system is typically most vulnerable toward the end of the economic cycle when excesses have built up and managing risks have been neglected. When you are not prepared for these events, shocks turn into crisis. I believe it is reasonable and prudent to expect that with the elevated levels of debt and tightening financial conditions as a result of the Fed raising interest rates, your investments need to be able to "adapt" to the changing market conditions.

This type of central bank intervention and debt accumulation coincides with what Alan Taylor of the University of Virginia calls the shift from the "Age of Money" to the "Age of Credit,"[44] a change he characterizes by an explosion of banks' balance sheets and a "mysterious" break in the fundamental macroeconomic relationship between the growth of money and the growth of the real economy.

With this "age of credit" and central bank intervention has come an ongoing succession of bubbles and crashes. In the late twentieth century there was the world-wide stock market bubble and the great crash of October 19, 1987; the savings and loan crisis of the 1980s; and the 1991 burst of the enormous Japanese real estate and stock market bubbles, along with the following "lost decades." But the cycle didn't end there. In 1994 and 1997 the emerging market bubble crashed; there was a crisis in long-term capital management (LTCM) in 1998; and if that weren't bad enough, the century ended with the dot-com bubble bursting in 2000. In the current century, our financial system was brought

---

[44] Taylor, Alan M., "The Great Leveraging." *World Scientific*. pp. 33-65, 2013. DOI: 10.1142/9789814520294_0004. Accessed 12 October 2018.

close to a virtual collapse in 2008 after the housing price bubble. Each euphoric bubble and crash was met with policies that fueled subsequent excesses, bubbles and crashes.

No matter where you come down on the different schools of economic thought, you should realize that the economy itself is a source of natural instability in your investments. Hyman Minsky, an American economist, outlined a hypothesis in his 1986 book, *Stabilizing an Unstable Economy*, which suggested that stability in financial markets engenders instability as a result of inherent tendencies in the financial system. In other words, stability is itself destabilizing. Excessive risk-taking, driven in part by over-optimistic assumptions about the level of risk, lead to market breakdowns.

INTEREST RATES AND THE ECONOMY

The economy runs on money, and one way to read the economy is the price of money—which is to say, interest rates. The law of supply and demand affects the price of money just as much as it does the price of eggs.

Absent any other information, the price of money depends on two things: How long you lend it for, and who you lend it to. Suppose your nephew asked you for a $10,000 loan. If he promised to pay you back in a week, you'd probably be willing to settle for a very low-interest loan—or, if you were feeling generous, a no-interest loan. If he wanted to borrow $1,000 for five years, however, you'd probably be inclined to charge a higher interest rate, because you would have lost the use of that money for a considerable time.

Now let's suppose your nephew did want a five-year loan for $10,000. He's a responsible guy with a steady job and bright prospects. He not only was an Eagle Scout, but rose to the rank of a major in Afghanistan. You'd probably be willing to give him a relatively low interest rate.

If your nephew had several arrests for theft and drugs, however, you might consider asking a higher interest rate, since he's been nothing but trouble since he was born, and there's a fair likelihood that the $10,000 is going to go to the race track or worse and in that case, you might want to reconsider loaning the money at all.

Loans to businesses or the government are guided by the same principles: You'd demand more on a loan to Argentina than to the U.S. Treasury, and you'd demand a higher rate on a 10-year loan to the U.S. government than a two-year loan.

The third part of all this is loan demand. In a healthy, growing economy, loan demand rises. People want to borrow to invest in their homes and businesses. As more people want to borrow, lenders raise their rates. As borrowing demand declines, lenders reduce their rates.

But it's not quite that simple. In order to make a loan, you need money to lend. In the nineteenth century, interest rates in New York would often spike in the fall as money flowed to the Midwest to pay farmers for their crops. (This was the beginning of October's terrible reputation for the stock market: High rates make stocks less attractive in comparison with bonds.)

While the Federal Reserve now smooths out banks' seasonal demand for currency, it can also raise and lower short-term interest rates by adding money to the system or by removing it. When the Fed wants to add money to the system, it buys government securities from major banks, which increases the amount of money they have to lend. When the Fed wants to remove money from the system, it sells government securities to banks, reducing their supply of cash.

When the Fed starts a campaign of raising interest rates, Wall

Street often shrugs it off. Rising rates, remember, are a sign of a healthy economy and growing loan demand. The Fed raised interest rates 17 times from 2004 though 2006, taking the key overnight Fed funds rate from 1.5% to 5.25%. The stock market gained 34% during that period.

But here's the catch: Sooner or later, the Fed often nudges rates up too far, stalling the economy and clobbering stocks. Part of this is because monetary policy works with about an eighteen-month lag. It takes that long for a single rate hike to have its full effect. As a result, the Fed is a bit like a farmer trying to water his crops from 150 miles away with a single faucet. Whenever he twists the faucet, he has to trudge out to the fields, check them, and trudge back. If the farmer lets the water run too long, the crops flood and die. If the farmer turns off the water entirely, the crops wilt. In short, raising and lowering interest rates is far from a science.

To make matters a bit more complicated, the Fed only controls the short side of interest rates—rates on loans with terms from one day to a year or so. The bond market controls the rest of the show. Longer-term interest rates reflect loan demand and lender sentiment. Sometimes, the Fed can be raising rates to slow down the economy, and the bond market can be lowering rates because they think the Fed is succeeding a bit too much.

The result is an inverted yield curve, where short-term rates, typically represented by the yield on the two-year Treasury note, are higher than the yield on the 10-year T-note. This doesn't happen often, but when it does, it's one of the most reliable signals that the economy is going to slide into recession. The yield curve went negative twice in 2006; the bear market began in October 2007, and the economy officially slid into recession in 2008. Similarly, the yield curve inverted in January 2000, and the economy went into recession in 2001.

At this writing, the yield curve is flat, but not yet inverted. The two-year T-note yields 2.82% and the 10-year T-note yields 3.09. What does that tell you? For one thing, you're not getting rewarded for tying up your money for a decade: You're better off with the two-year note. And, while a flat yield curve doesn't have the ominous cachet that an inverted yield curve does, it means you should keep a close eye on the yield curve. You don't want to ignore an inverted yield curve.

TARIFFS AND TRADE WARS

A tariff is a tax on imports and can result in a trade war. A trade war is just what it sounds like: when countries try to attack each other's trade with taxes (tariffs) and quotas. Typically, one country will raise tariffs, which is a tax on imported goods, causing the other to respond in what becomes a tit-for-tat escalation. The companies that import goods pay the tariffs, not the companies that export them. The result is higher prices at home for imported goods.

For example, say an American retailer buys 100 backpacks from China for $5 apiece, or $500. The U.S. tariff rate for backpacks is 10 percent. The retailer would have to pay a $50 tariff on the shipment of backpacks, raising the total price from $500 to $550 and would likely need to pass the increased cost on to consumers. The increased price of the backpacks could discourage consumers from purchasing that item, thereby reducing demand for that product and hurting both the importer and the exporter. On the other hand, domestic producers and retailers of backpacks could benefit from less foreign competition, as consumers look for a cheaper backpack to buy. Trade wars can damage economies, raise inflation, and increase political tensions.

The underlying idea of a tariff is that the tax on the items coming into the country will become more expensive and people are less likely to buy them. Instead, they will opt to buy cheaper local products instead, thereby boosting their country's own economy. Trade wars can begin for a variety of reasons, including if one country perceives another country's trading practices to be unfair, which is the case with the U.S. and China. History suggests that tariffs typically lead to higher costs for consumers.

One of the major problems with China is that its innovation is largely borrowed technology.

Alan Greenspan

At midnight on Thursday, July 5, 2018, the United States officially entered into a trade war (some prefer to say trade dispute) with China. The U.S. placed a 25% tariff on more than 800 Chinese products, with an estimated cost of $34 billion. China immediately responded with a series of tariffs of their own, insisting that President Donald Trump had started "the biggest trade war in economic history."

The Trump administration is hitting other countries with tariffs as well. These additional countries include the European Union, Canada, Mexico, South Korea, Argentina, and Brazil—and that list may expand. As the U.S. takes a more aggressive approach and affected countries retaliate, tensions are building. The dispute mechanism of the World Trade Organization (WTO) is facing the most critical period in its history. Very few economists expect this to end well and do not believe it will improve Americans' overall economic well-being. Some economists suggest that imposing tariffs on steel, for example, will increase prices and harm the U.S. consumer and other Americans working in manufacturing industries that utilize steel. On the other hand, the potential winners of the steel tariffs are some of the American steel and aluminum-producing industries.

I bring up the issue of tariffs to highlight the potential impact on investors and their portfolios, and how the Adaptive Investment Portfolio can help prepare investors for the changes that may occur. Tariff escalation can shock investor confidence. There can be disruptions in bilateral trade and global supply chains, and that can have an effect on portfolios. There may be uncertainty across large sectors of the economy as more people start worrying about the impact on items such as automobiles, washing machines, and technology. It is for those reasons that portfolios need the ability to adapt to the rapidly changing global trade environment.

DEMOGRAPHICS

What you and I buy every day drives the U.S. economy and economic growth. Consumer spending includes everyday household items, large and small, and includes services, too. About two-thirds of consumer spending is on services such as real estate, healthcare, and financial services (banking, investments, and insurance). The other one-third of our spending is on goods, also referred to as durable goods, such as washing machines, cars, groceries, and clothing.

Consumer spending is the single most important force driving the U.S. economy and represents about 70 percent of American Gross Domestic Product (GDP). As discussed above, when consumer spending increases, the result is investment and economic growth. When consumer spending decreases, the result is economic contraction.

The demography of the population hugely affects the size and composition of the labor force, and thus economic development. But how does demography, or the make-up of the population as defined by age, gender, race, and ethnicity, affect the sustainable pace of GDP growth for the United States? Let's refer to spending wave theory[45], which studies the economic effect of children coming of age and departing the home. When a society experiences a high level of such family change, then an economic decline follows from reduced overall spending. On the other end of the age wave are the Baby Boomers, those born between 1946 and 1964. In their day, the Baby Boom generation was a powerful economic force, with nearly 77 million members. They represented 40 percent of the nation's population. They were so significant that in 1966, Time magazine declared that the generation 25 and under would be its "Persons of the Year." A Life magazine story in 1958 declared that "kids" were a "built-in recession cure."

But according to the Bureau of Labor Statistics, income and expenditures have a life cycle pattern that peaks between the ages of 45-54.[46] Today, the oldest Baby Boomers are already in their seventies. They are not only spending less, they have also downsized their family homes and are now taking investment distributions and selling stocks. By 2030, about one in five Americans will be older than sixty-five, and some experts believe that the aging of the population will place a strain on the social welfare system.

---

[45] Siegel, Jeremy J., *Stocks for the Long Run: The Definitive Guide to Financial Market Returns and Long-Term Investment Strategies, 3rd.* McGraw-Hill, 2002.

[46] Foster, Ann C. "Consumer Expenditures Vary by Age." *Bureau of Labor Statistics*, 2015, vol. 4, no. 14, 2015. https://www.bls.gov/opub/btn/volume-4/consumer-expenditures-vary-by-age.htm. Accessed 12 October 2018.

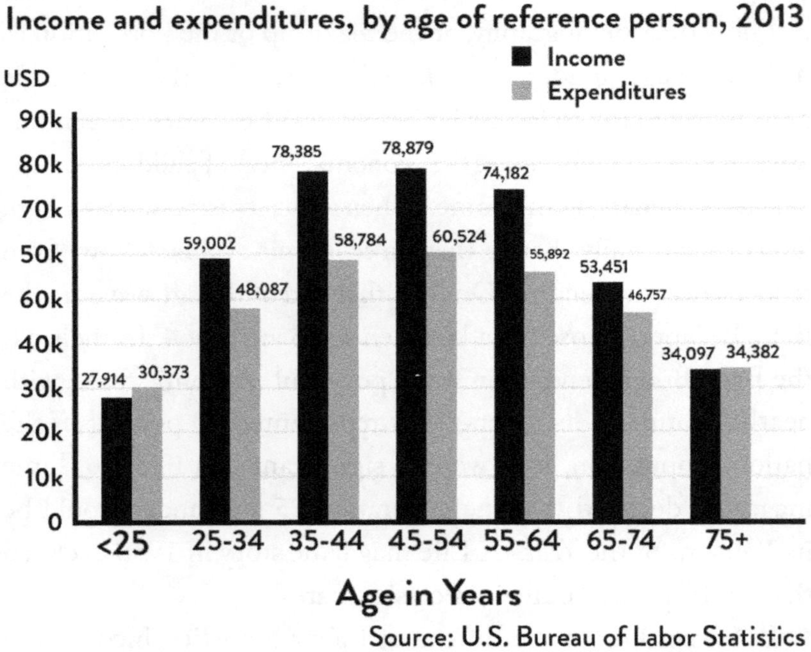

Figure 10.[47]

The United States is not only experiencing an aging trend, it is also undergoing a decline in the fertility rate, which has been falling since 2007. Fertility determines population in the long term, and lower numbers can mean less available labor and less economic growth, which leads to downturns in the economy. These demographic changes, in particular their effect on the labor supply and consumption, are headwinds that will likely result in a measurable slowdown in macroeconomic performance (Figure 12).

---

[47] Foster, Ann C. "Consumer expenditures vary by age." Bureau of Labor Statistics, vol. 4, no. 14, 2015. https://www.bls.gov/opub/btn/volume-4/consumer-expenditures-vary-by-age.htm. Accessed 24 October 2018.

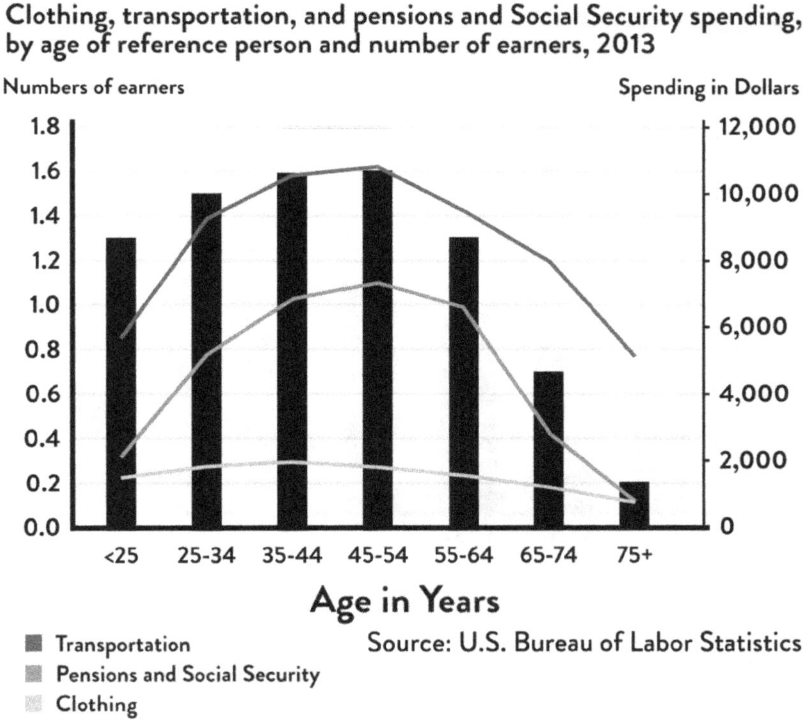
Clothing, transportation, and pensions and Social Security spending, by age of reference person and number of earners, 2013
Numbers of earners
Spending in Dollars
1.8
1.6
1.4
1.2
1.0
0.8
0.6
0.4
0.2
0.0
12,000
10,000
8,000
6,000
4,000
2,000
0
<25
25-34
35-44
45-54
55-64
65-74
75+
Age in Years
Transportation
Pensions and Social Security
Clothing
Source: U.S. Bureau of Labor Statistics

Figure 11.[48]

[48] Ibid.

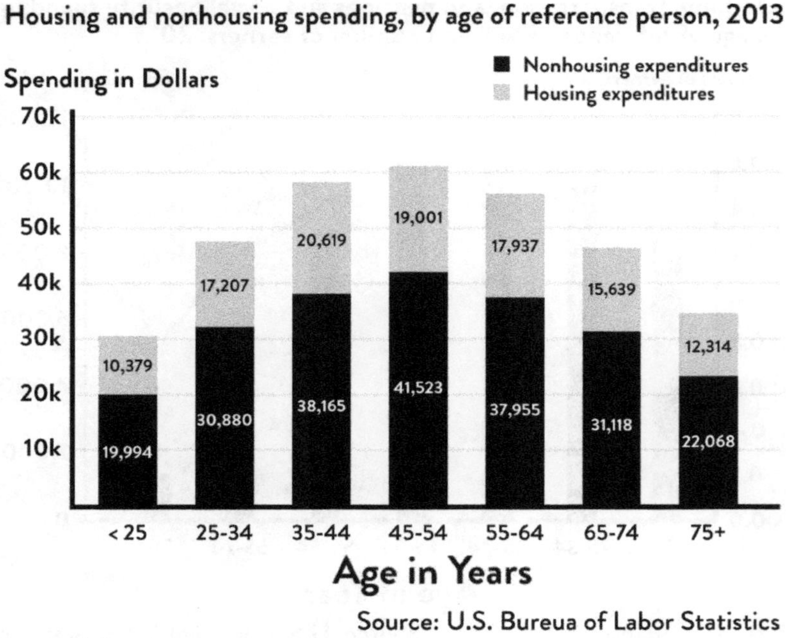

Figure 12.[49]

PENSIONS AND SOCIAL SECURITY

The earlier Baby Boomers had the benefit of working for companies that provided a traditional defined-benefit pension plan for them in their retirement. Companies contributed to pension plans, and they guaranteed that retirees would receive a monthly check for as long as they lived. But pensions, once an integral part of retirement

[49] Ibid.

planning, have been on the decline for the past twenty-five years.[50] In the 1980s there were 112,000 pension plans still available in the United States. In 2015 there were only 45,672[51]—a drop of over 59 percent. While companies used to manage pension assets for employees, providing for workers during retirement, that responsibility has been shifted to the employees through non-guaranteed, self-directed accounts.

Some of the larger U.S. corporations that do still offer pensions find that they are seriously underwater, and as the Baby Boomer wave of retirement kicks into full gear, this problem is only getting worse. According to Morningstar, an independent financial research group, most state pension plans continue to be underfunded. Decreased funding and increasing liabilities since the 2008 recession continue to put pressure on local and state pension plans, in some cases leading to bankruptcy.[52]

Between 2015 and 2025, the U.S. population as a whole will grow 8 percent, but the number of people between the ages of 70 and 84 will increase by 50 percent. Currently, the number of retirees is increasing by about 1.2 million a year, about three times more than a decade ago.[53]

Due to this shift in demographics, there will be a significant

---

[50] Butrica, Barbara, Howard M. Iams, Karen E. Smith, and Eric J. Toder. "The Disappearing Defined Benefit Pension and its Potential Impact on Retirement Incomes of Baby Boomer." *Social Security Bulletin*. vol. 69, no. 3, 2009. https://www.ssa.gov/policy/docs/ssb/v69n3/v69n3p1.html. Accessed 12 October 2018.

[51] "Private Pension Plan Bulletin Historical Tables and Graphs 1975-2015." Employee Benefits Security Administration. United States Department of Labor.
https://www.dol.gov/sites/default/files/ebsa/researchers/statistics/retirement-bulletins/private-pension-plan-bulletin-historical-tables-and-graphs.pdf. Accessed 12 October 2018.

[52] "Public Pensions in the United States." Ballotpedia. https://ballotpedia.org/Public_pensions_in_the_United_States. Accessed 12 October 2018.

[53] "Demographic Trends and Demand Shifts: 2016-2025." *The Conference Board*. https://www.conference-board.org/demographic-trends-consumption/ Accessed 12 October 2018.

impact on healthcare spending. "Over the next decade, health spending will grow 15 percent due to demographic trends alone, compared with 8 percent for total consumption spending," according to Gad Levanon, chief North American economist at the Conference Board.

Social Security is in the same situation, but on a much larger scale. The Social Security system, an important social insurance program that many Americans have come to rely on, is critically underfunded. This at a time just as it is entering a phase of extremely high liabilities as Baby Boomers retire en masse. In 1945[54] there were almost 42 workers supporting one retiree; but by 1970, that number had fallen to just 3.7 workers supporting one retiree. By 2020 that ratio is projected to be 2.2 workers supporting one retiree, and down to almost 2 to 1 by 2030 (Figure 13). The trustees of the Social Security Trust Fund project that it will be depleted by 2034 unless there is meaningful entitlement reform.

While demographic trends and the strains on Social Security create a future that is uncertain for many retirees, a solid retirement plan is now more important than ever. Retirees must consider the knowns and unknowns while taking steps to offset the potential risk of reduced or eliminated benefits. By working to develop an effective savings plan and an adaptive investment strategy, you can still achieve a comfortable retirement without depending on Social Security.

[54] Note on the data: At the inception of Social Security in 1935, there were few beneficiaries and a lot of workers. https://www.mercatus.org/publication/how-many-workers-support-one-social-security-retiree

How Many Workers Support One Social Security Retiree?

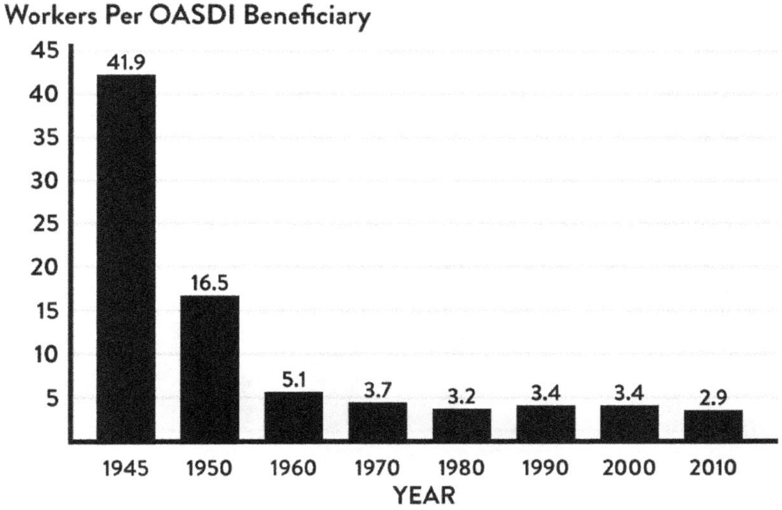

Source: 2012 OASDI Trustee Report, Table IV.B2., www.ssa.gov, accessed May 21, 2012. Data note: The Trustee Report provides data from 1945 and onward. Prior estimates are unavailable. Produced by Veronique du Rugy Mercatus Center at George Mason Univ.

Figure 13.[55]

[55] de Rugy, Veronique. "How Many Workers Support One Social Security Retiree?" Mercatus Center, George Mason University. 22 May 2012. https://www.mercatus.org/publication/how-many-workers-support-one-social-security-retiree. Accessed 24 October 2018.

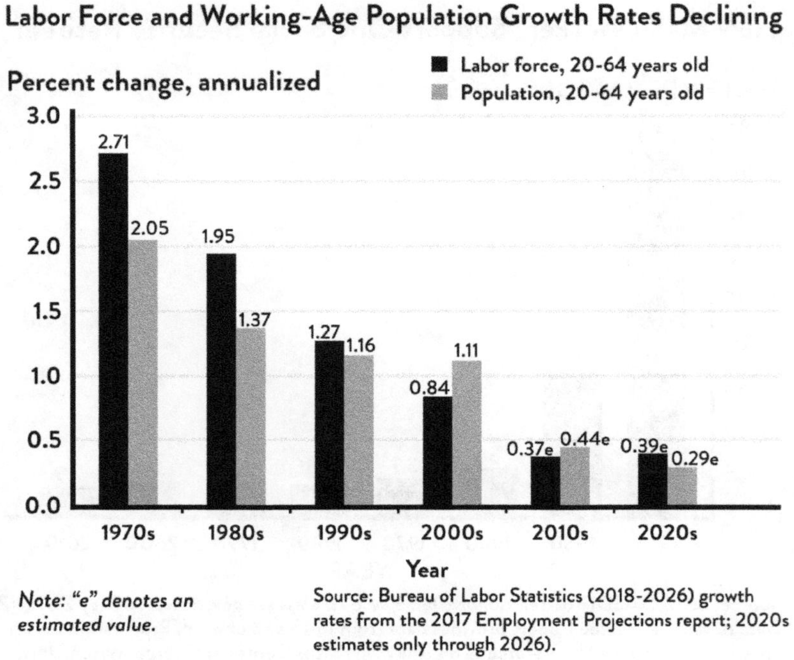

Figure 14.[56]

[56] Kaplan, Robert. "Where We Stand: Assessment of Economic Conditions and Implications for Monetary Policy." *Federal Reserve Bank of Dallas*. 21 August 2018. https://www.dallasfed.org/news/speeches/kaplan/2018/rsk180821.aspx. Accessed 24 October 2018.

U.S. population, by age, selected years 1950-2080

Year	Population (thousands)				% 65 and older
	All ages	Under 20	20-64	65+	
			Historical		
1950	160,118	54,466	92,841	12,811	8
1970	214,765	80,684	113,158	20,923	10
1990	260,458	75,060	153,368	32,029	12
2005	302,323	83,963	181,457	36,902	12
			Historical		
2020	339,269	87,547	198,213	53,510	16
2040	376,856	92,268	207,416	77,172	20
2060	402,079	96,760	218,777	86,543	22
2080	428,214	101,159	230,137	96,918	23

Source: Board of Trustees (2006, Table V.A2) and author's calculations

Figure 15.[57]

[57] Reznik, Gayle L., and Dave Shoffner and David A. Weaver. "Coping with the Demographic Challenge: Fewer Children and Living Longer." *Social Security Bulletin*, vol. 66, no. 4. 2005/2006. https://www.ssa.gov/policy/docs/ssb/v66n4/v66n4p37.html. Accessed 24 October 2018.

CHAPTER 5

THE FEDERAL RESERVE

I know you think you understand what you thought I said, but I'm not sure you realize that what you heard is not what I meant.
- Alan Greenspan

Any serious discussion about the economy and the markets must include the Federal Reserve System—or the Fed—and the role it plays. The Federal Reserve is always right there on the front lines, directly affecting everything revolving around the U.S. economy, and even the global one. The Federal Reserve is the central bank of the United States and was created on December 23, 1913, and opened its doors in 1914.

Prior to the establishment of the Fed, the country had a series of financial crises. These crises would sometimes turn into panics, which resulted in people running to their banks to withdraw all of their deposits—often causing those banks to collapse, taking peoples' savings with them. Before federal deposit insurance, banks paid depositors what they could when the bank failed—often just pennies on the dollar.

One crisis in particular, the Panic of 1907 in the U.S. banking industry and stock market, had a devastating effect on the economy. This financial crisis took place over a three-week period during which the New York Stock Exchange fell almost 50 percent from the previous year's high.

Many believed that the big New York banks, known at the time as the Money Trust, had been causing crashes, and then profiting on them. They bought up stocks from shaken investors on the cheap and then sold them for huge profits just days or weeks afterward. A failed attempt by the big New York banks to corner the market on the stock of the United Copper Company triggered the panic. The panic caused runs when a number of New York banks removed liquidity[58] from the market and there was a loss of confidence among depositors. The Panic of 1907 was a devastating event that eventually spread across the nation as many state and local banks and businesses entered bankruptcy.

In 1908 Congress established the National Monetary Commission to investigate the crisis and propose banking reforms that would provide solutions and prevent future panics. A central figure in the creation of the American central bank was a U.S. senator from Rhode Island, Nelson W. Aldrich, the father-in-law of John D. Rockefeller, Jr. Aldrich was appointed chairman of the commission which ultimately led to the creation of the Federal Reserve System.[59, 60]

The idea of a central bank was formulated at a secret meeting in 1910 at an exclusive men's club on a secluded island off the

---

[58] Liquidity is cash, cash equivalents and other assets that can be easily converted into cash (liquidated). In the case of a market, a stock or a commodity, the extent to which there are sufficient buyers and sellers to ensure that a few buy or sell orders would not move prices very much.

[59] "Born of a Panic: Forming the Fed System." *The Region*. 1 August 1988. https://www.minneapolisfed.org/publications/the-region/born-of-a-panic-forming-the-fed-system. Accessed 14 October 2018.

[60] Tucker, Abigail. "The Financial Panic of 1907: Running from History." *Smithsonian Magazine*. 9 October 2008. https://www.smithsonianmag.com/history/the-financial-panic-of-1907-running-from-history-82176328/. Accessed 14 October 2018.

Georgia coast where J.P. Morgan was a member. Aldrich and executives, representing the firms of J.P. Morgan, Rockefeller and Kuhn, Loeb & Co., the National City Bank of New York, and the First National Bank of New York, planned on a ten-day retreat at Jekyll Island.[61] The meeting participants traveled to the island pretending to be duck hunters. The meeting was so secretive that the participants did not even acknowledge that it took place until the 1930s. It was at this week-long meeting that they wrote what became the first draft of the Federal Reserve Act. At the time of its creation, the Fed was seen as having a somewhat limited function. The purpose was to restructure America's financial system and protect the safety and soundness of the banking system and to be a lender of last resort, providing liquidity to banks in times of crises.[62]

One of the attendees at the secret Jekyll Island meeting was Frank A. Vanderlip, president of the National City Bank of New York. In his 1935 autobiography, *From Farmboy to Financier*, he wrote this:

> Despite my views about the value to society of greater publicity for the affairs of corporations, there was an occasion, near the close of 1910, when I was as secretive, indeed, as furtive as any conspirator. None of us who participated felt that we were conspirators; on the contrary we felt we were engaged in a patriotic work. We were trying to plan a mechanism

[61] Whithouse, Michael."Paul Warburg's Crusade to Establish a Central Bank in the United States." *Federal Reserve Bank of Minneapolis*. 1 May 1989. https://www.minneapolisfed.org/publications/the-region/paul-warburgs-crusade-to-establish-a-central-bank-in-the-united-states. Accessed 14 October 2018.

[62] Bagwell, Tyler E. "The Jekyll Island Duck Hunt that Created the Federal Reserve." *Jeckyl Island History*. http://jekyllislandhistory.com. Accessed 14 October 2018.

> that would correct the weaknesses of our banking system as revealed under the strains and pressures of the panic of 1907. I do not feel it is any exaggeration to speak of our secret expedition to Jekyll Island as the occasion of the actual conception of what eventually became the Federal Reserve System. . . . Discovery, we knew, simply must not happen, or else all our time and effort would be wasted. If it were to be exposed publicly that our particular group had gotten together and written a banking bill, that bill would have no chance whatever of passage by Congress. Yet, who was there in Congress who might have drafted a sound piece of legislation dealing with the purely banking problem with which we were concerned?[63]

There was opposition to the Aldrich Plan, and U.S. Sen. Robert M. La Follette, Sr. (R-Wisconsin) and U.S. Rep. Charles Lindbergh, Sr.[64] (R-Minnesota) both spoke out against the favoritism they claimed that the bill granted Wall Street. In response, Rep. Arsène Pujo (D-Louisiana) obtained Congressional authorization to form and chair a subcommittee within the House Committee Banking Committee to investigate the hearings on the alleged "Money Trust." The finally subcommittee issued this report.[65]

---

[63] Vanderlip, Frank A. and Boyden Sparkes. *From Farm Boy to Financier.* D. Appleton-Century Co., 1935/ as quoted in deCarbonnel, Eric. "Frank Vanderlip And The Creation Of The Federal Reserve." 19 June 2009. *Market Skeptics.* http://www.marketskeptics.com/2009/06/frank-vanderlip-and-creation-of-federal.html. Accessed 16 October 2018.

[64] This is the father of the famous American aviator, Charles Lindbergh, Jr.

[65] "U.S. Congress, Excerpts from the Report of the Committee Appointed to Investigate the Concentration of Money and Credit, House Report No. 1593, 3 vols. (Washington, D.C., 1913), III: pp. 55–56, 89, 129, 140." https://babel.hathitrust.org/cgi/pt?id=mdp.39015056056057;view=1up;seq=3. Accessed 14 October 2018.

> If by a 'money trust' is meant an established and well-defined identity and community of interest between a few leaders of finance...which has resulted in a vast and growing concentration of control of money and credit in the hands of a comparatively few men...the condition thus described exists in this country today...To us the peril is manifest...When we find...the same man a director in a half dozen or more banks and trust companies all located in the same section of the same city, doing the same class of business and with a like set of associates similarly situated all belonging to the same group and representing the same class of interests, all further pretense of competition is useless ...[66]

Once the bill was ultimately drafted and introduced by Aldrich, and after months of hearings, amendments, and debates, the Federal Reserve Act passed Congress in December 1913. Sen. Aldrich pledged all participants of the Jekyll Island meeting to secrecy, both from the public and from the rest of the government. Despite that pledge, three years after the Federal Reserve Act was passed, the importance of the meeting was revealed when a journalist wrote an article about the hunting trip revealing secretive details.[67]

I would like to pause here to remind you of why this information about the Federal Reserve is important for you and your investment portfolio. The Fed is the puppet master behind the economic curtain and can stimulate economic growth with easy money policies or, at the flip of a switch, can tighten economic

---

[66] Johnson, Roger. *Historical Beginnings... The Federal Reserve*. Federal Reserve Bank of Boston. 1999. https://www.bostonfed.org/publications/economic-education/historical-beginnings.aspx. Accessed 14 October 2018.

[67] Forbes, Bertie M. *Men who are making America*. B. C. Forbes Publishing Co., 1922.

conditions by taking away the easy money punch bowl in an attempt to prevent the economic party from getting out of hand. Economists and analysts have concern about how the Fed will reverse the massive QE (Quantitative Easing)[68] program which has been the major force driving the powerful bull market in stocks. Using history as a guide, we know that the U.S. central bank tends to raise interest rates too high when trying to wind the party down, causing recessions and stock market declines (which is a current risk to the market). The better you understand the effects of their actions, the better you will be able to use that information as a guide to adapt to the changing market conditions with the conviction that is required to achieve higher risk adjusted returns.

To comprehend the workings of the central bank mechanism, one first needs to know about the U.S. fractional reserve banking system, which allows banks to create credit and make loans from the money they hold in the form of customer deposits. All banks have what is called a "reserve requirement," meaning they must keep a percentage of the money in reserve to meet customer withdrawals. We all know that when you deposit a check, the money doesn't just stay in your bank's vault until you need it. They lend the money and make investments with most of it, which is how they generate their income. The basic idea is that not every depositor will look to withdraw his deposits at the same time. The percentage of deposits that the banks are required to keep on hand varies, but let's say 20 percent, for the sake of this example. If a customer comes in to deposit $100, the bank can lend out or invest $80, but is required to keep $20 of the customer deposit as reserves (The Fed sets the reserve requirement).

[68] Quantitative Easing (QE), also known as large-scale asset purchases, is an expansionary monetary policy whereby a central bank buys predetermined amounts of government bonds or other financial assets in order to stimulate the economy and increase liquidity.

By loaning out 80 percent of deposits at prevailing market interest rates, or investing in speculative projects, banks create revenue, but they also expand the economy and money supply. This practice results in what is called the multiplier effect—because it literally multiplies—the money supply. In the example above, when the bank loans out $80 of the $100 that was deposited, the $80 is then deposited by the new customer into another bank which in turn must keep 20 percent in reserves, but can loan the other 80 percent. This cycle continues as more people deposit money and more banks continue lending it, until finally the $100 initially deposited creates a total of $500 in deposits.

When the banks look for ways to loan or invest the money they have taken in from deposits, they are supposed to invest it prudently. Periodically, however, bankers decide they want to be growth companies and invest in more speculative or risky projects. This is nearly always a bad idea. As this continues and the amount of money the bank has invested grows larger, the risks increase. Although the bank has assets, it may not be able to quickly turn those assets into cash, making them vulnerable to loss. In system-wide events, banking capital reserves are insufficient to support all of the possible claims on deposits. As fear spreads, depositors demand their money back, causing the potential for bank runs.[69]

The fear of bank runs is not unfounded. American history includes well-known examples of such runs, which contributed to a collapse of confidence in the entire financial system. They occurred every decade after the Civil War and even after the Federal Reserve System was established. By far the worst panics occurred between 1930 and 1933, when over one-third of the nation's banks failed. Each banking crisis has led to greater centralization, and the

[69] A bank run (also known as a run on the bank) occurs when a large number of people withdraw their money from a bank, because they believe the bank may cease to function in the near future.

burden of liability for reckless speculation falls on the shoulders of the taxpayer as the public bails them out. In a capitalist economy, the prospect of failure should impose prudence and discipline on the banks in order to avoid crisis.[70]

In addition to being the lender of last resort, the role of the Fed has expanded, and it now uses monetary policy—primarily interest rates—to help promote economic well-being. A few of the main monetary policy tools are as follows:

1. **The discount rate**: The discount rate is the interest rate charged to commercial banks and other depository institutions on loans they receive from their regional Federal Reserve Bank's lending facility.
2. **Reserve requirements**: This is how much a bank has to hold in reserves. The Fed uses the tool to control how much banks can lend.
3. **Open Market Operations (OMO)**: Listen up, because this one is important. You might have heard how the Fed is buying assets in a program known as Quantitative Easing (QE), and we'll get to that later. OMOs are similar, and have been the longstanding program by which the Fed implements monetary policy. The Fed has used OMOs—the purchase or sale of government securities on the open market as a means to adjust the federal funds rate to a specified Fed target. The federal funds rate is a metric that controls interbank loans.

When the Fed reduces the federal funds rate, as it did between 2007 and 2008, other short-term rates follow. Low interest rates

[70] Rolnick, Arthur J. "The alarming costs of preventing bank runs." *FedGazette*. 1 April 1991. *Federal Reserve Bank of Minneapolis*. https://www.minneapolisfed.org/publications/fedgazette/the-alarming-costs-of-preventing-bank-runs. Accessed 18 October 2018.

(cheap money) incentivizes banks to lend more freely (credit expansion), and encourages borrowers to take on more debt or refinance old debt at lower rates, theoretically speeding up the economy.

It is interesting to note here that every financial bubble has been associated with the expansion of credit. In the book, *Manias, Panics, and Crashes*, by Charles P. Kindleberger, professor emeritus of internal economics at MIT, and Robert Z. Aliber, professor emeritus of international economics and finance at the University of Chicago, wrote, "Speculative manias gather speed through expansion of money and credit. Most expansions of money and credit do not lead to a mania; there are many more economic expansions than manias, but every mania has been associated with the expansion of credit."[71]

I make this point because of the extraordinary policy response from the Federal Reserve as a counter to the 2008 financial crisis: bailing out the big banks. It was something the likes of which the world has never seen before. The result has been a fantastic run-up in asset prices across the board. While the actions of the Fed did prevent the entire system from failing, they have also pushed people into riskier investments in search of higher returns to overcome the lowest interest rates ever seen.

Speculation and risk-taking behavior are seemingly risk-free, as long as everybody, particularly large, too-big-to-fail institutions, believes that the Fed is there to bail them out if needed. If the Fed feels that the financial system is getting overheated, it can raise the federal funds rate to slow things down.

The financial crises of 2008 had caused a collapse in the value of bank assets. They were suddenly insolvent, and therefore pre-

---

[71] Kindleberger, Charles P. and Robert Z. Aliber. *Manias, Panics, and Crashes: A History of Financial Crisis*. Palgrave Macmillan, 2015.

sented a systemic risk to the economy. The Fed's response to the crisis was to lower interest rates, ultimately to zero, in order to increase the prices of the troubled assets, which did indeed occur. Since then, we have had a boom in the value of assets across the board—from stocks and bonds to property, oil paintings, and classic cars. There is a sense of invulnerability as a result of the extraordinarily loose monetary policy.

Now the Fed has reversed course and has begun to unwind the easy money policy era by raising interest rates, which officially started in 2015. If asset prices have risen so sharply as a result of the Fed's low interest rate policies, it is completely reasonable to expect asset prices to reverse course as interest rates continue to rise.

The Fed today has what is known as a "dual mandate," which is to "promote effectively the goals of maximum employment, stable prices, and moderate long term interest rates".[72] The concern that Fed watchers have with the dual mandate is that if the Fed is concerned with full employment, it has an incentive to keep interest rates low to juice up the economy. If rates are kept too low, for too long, asset bubbles can form. In 2001 we had a stock market bubble. In 2007, we had a housing bubble. Now there are signs that we have an "everything bubble" as the record low interest rates have inflated almost all asset prices through the roof. As we have learned from history, bubbles can lead to the kinds of banking crises the Fed was originally charged with preventing.

In a study by economists George Selgin, William D. Lastrapes, and Lawrence H. White, of the conservative Cato Institute, they state the following:

---

[72] Steelman, Aaron. "The Federal Reserve's 'Dual Mandate': The Evolution of an Idea." *The Federal Reserve Bank of Richmond,* no. 11-12, 2011. https://www.richmondfed.org/publications/research/economic_brief/2011/eb_11-12. Accessed 14 October 2018.

> 1) The Fed's full history (1914 to present) has been characterized by more rather than fewer symptoms of monetary and macroeconomic instability than the decades leading to the Fed's establishment. 2) While the Fed's performance has undoubtedly improved since World War II, even its postwar performance has not clearly surpassed that of its undoubtedly flawed predecessor, the National Banking system, before World War I. 3) Some proposed alternative arrangements might plausibly do better than the Fed as presently constituted. We conclude that the need for a systemic exploration of alternatives to the established monetary system is as pressing today as it was a century ago.[73]

In practice, this is a fundamental source of periodic economic instability. In a study published in 2006 by Spanish economist Jesus Huerta de Soto[74], he places blame on the institution of fractional reserve banking. The system works as long as people do not attempt to withdraw all their money all at once. When a large number of customers withdraw their deposits simultaneously over concerns about the bank's solvency, it faces a choice of either going bankrupt or suspending payments. Banks can turn to other banks for liquidity, but when the panic is system-wide, they all turn to the government.

The key point the author of the study makes is that the conventional premise—that an unregulated financial system leads to crisis and only the government can control it—is not accurate.

---

[73] George Selgin is a professor at the Terry College of Business at the University of Georgia, and a senior fellow at the Cato Institute. William D. Lastrapes is a professor at the Terry College of Business at the University of Georgia. Lawrence H. White is a professor at the Department of Economics at George Mason University, and an adjunct scholar at the Cato Institute.

[74] de Soto, Jesus Huerta. *Money, Bank Credit, Economic Cycles.* Ludwig von Mises Institute, 2006.

Huerta de Soto suggests that in fact there is far more reason to believe the contrary, that it is government control that distorts the financial system and creates excessive instability.

As history has shown, the economy moves in boom and bust cycles and the Fed's monetary policies are a key driver. As we are now very late in the current economic cycle, debt levels are stretched and asset prices are at nosebleed levels. Investors need to stay alert. The stakes are high, and the possibility for policy errors are multiplying. The effects of central bank policy on the markets can be dramatic and swift so investors must be agile and adaptive.

CHAPTER 6

THE MARKETS

Everyone has a plan until they get punched in the face.
- Mike Tyson

I am an optimist by nature. That is not just my disposition; it's also my personal view on things as an investment professional—and for good reason. We live in an incredible time. Our quality of life is amazing. Advancements in medical care allow us to live longer and healthier lives than ever before. New technology—from cars that can park themselves to one-click shopping on Amazon to real-time video chatting—have opened up a whole new world, making our lives richer and more interesting than ever before. This is an incredibly great time to be alive.

Having said all of that, we as investors want to be informed and aware of periodic market factors that can have a cyclical effect on our investments. Some of these, like the presidential election cycle, are fairly straightforward and the impact is easy to understand. Others, such as the miserable market record for the month of September, are not as easy to figure out. Since 1950, September has been the worst month of the year for the Dow and the S&P 500, according to the *Stock Trader's Almanac*. While market cycles are not as reliable as the seasons, they do appear with enough regularity to justify our attention, as they have the potential to seriously affect your portfolio. You should be aware of these cycles because they also present opportunity. The Adaptive Investment Portfolio is designed not only to shield your investments from their ill effects, but also to take advantage of those opportunities as they arise.

To understand market cycles, you need to know how the markets themselves work. Because stocks and bonds make up the largest part of most investment portfolios, it is important to have a general knowledge of how they operate as well. Let's start with stocks. When businesses need long-term capital, they sell interests in the company by issuing stock. When you buy a stock, you own a piece of the company, and can even have a say—albeit tiny—in how the company conducts business.

Unless you buy stock at the initial public offering, when the company first makes it available to the public, you buy stock from another interested seller. For that, you need an exchange. The New York Stock Exchange (NYSE) is the nation's oldest. A group of twenty-four brokers originally agreed on commissions and other trading practices under a buttonwood tree in New York on May 17, 1792. (We call them sycamore trees these days.) At first, traders mostly dealt with government bonds.

The exchange moved several times from its original home at a coffee house and eventually settled at 11 Wall Street. Over time, other exchanges emerged, such as the American Stock Exchange—called "The Curb" because traders shouted orders from the sidewalk to traders on Wall Street. The Nasdaq, which is an acronym for the National Association of Securities Dealers Automated Quotations, emerged in 1971 and is the second-largest exchange in the world by market capitalization, behind the NYSE.

Nicknamed "The Big Board" while still located on Wall Street, the New York Stock Exchange is currently owned by Intercontinental Exchange, an American holding company. Today the NYSE, by far the world's largest stock exchange, trades about 2,800 company stocks, and handles approximately 1.46 billion trades each day, as well as hundreds of exchange traded funds (ETFs), and even some bonds.

In many ways, the stock market is the optimist of the two markets, while bonds are more the pessimist. Stocks move up on the expectation of increased earnings, which, in turn, are typically a byproduct of a booming economy. When times are good, companies can expand, build new factories, increase dividends, or buy back shares of their own stock. The stock market thrives on good news.

Bonds, on the other hand, are only happy when it rains. Bonds are long-term IOUs issued by corporations, states, municipal entities, and the federal government. When you buy a bond, you're a lender. You're lending the issuer money, collecting interest for a set period of time, and getting your principal back when the bond matures. On old-time bonds, investors were given an actual certificate with small detachable coupons on them. To get your interest payment, you'd have to clip the coupon and mail it to the issuer. While bond payments are electronic today, the set interest rate on a bond is still called the "coupon rate."

The bond market is big, really big. According to some estimates, the bond market now exceeds $100 trillion, while the S&P and Dow Jones Industrial Average (DOW) indices are worth about $64 trillion. Trading volume in bonds is also much greater than the trading volume of stocks, with nearly $700 billion in bonds traded on a daily basis compared to less than $200 billion per day in volume for stocks, according to data from industry group Securities Industry and Financial Markets Association (SIFMA).

And where is the bond exchange? There isn't a physical one. It's a network of banks and traders, linked by telephones and the Internet.

Why is the bond market so pessimistic? Well, it's complicated. First, most bonds' interest rate—the coupon rate—are fixed, which is why we call the bond market the fixed-income market. When you buy a bond, you're agreeing to an interest rate, and you can't demand more from the issuer.

Because bond interest rates are fixed, traders can, instead, bid the price of the bond itself up or down. Suppose you own a $10,000 bond that yields 5 percent. In a year or so, you decide to sell your bond. Unfortunately, newly-issued bonds yield 6 percent, and traders turn up their noses at your measly 5 percent bond. To pique their interest, you'd have to drop the price of your bond below $10,000 so that its yield—the interest payment divided by price—is equal to 6 percent. (Of course, you can hold your bond to maturity and won't take any loss at all.) Bond prices fall when interest rates rise, and they rise when interest rates fall.

The bond market's reputation for gloom stems from its dislike of higher interest rates. In the normal course of events, interest rates rise when the economy is booming, and rates fall when the economy is faltering. This is why you'll see headlines like "Bond market tumbles on news of record low unemployment," and "Bond market stages massive rally on disappointing GDP number." And that's also why most portfolios have a bond component; bonds often rise when stocks fall, and vice versa.

Finally, because bond investors are lenders, they must keep an eye on the creditworthiness of the bond issuer. Credit risk refers to the possibility that the bond issuer is going to shuffle off to Palookaville and miss making its payments. Bond investors will cut a bond's price dramatically if the issuer shows any signs of faltering. They raise a bond's price if its credit is improving. Junk bonds, which Wall Street prefers to call high-yield bonds, have high yields because their credit is dinged—and are therefore a riskier investment than Treasury securities, which have virtually no credit risk.

The current bond market environment has changed and it is not like it has been in the recent past. The yield on the bellwether 10-year Treasury note had been falling since 1981, until July 2016, when the 10-year yield made a record low of 1.37%. As you recall, falling rates means rising bond prices, meaning the bond market had been in a thirty-five year bull market from 1981 to 2016.

We can say definitively that we are now in a new era of generally-rising interest rates, in addition to higher volatility for the bond market. The average yield on the bellwether 10-year Treasury note has been between 6.2 percent since 1962; it's just above 3 percent as of this writing (September 2018).

Not all bonds react the same way to rising rates. To understand why that is, you need to know about bond maturity and duration. A bond's maturity is simply the term of the bond. A ten-year bond typically pays interest throughout its lifetime, with a return of the principal when the bond "matures" at year ten. As a bond ages, its maturity shortens. For example, a ten-year bond today is a nine-year bond one year from now.

A ten-year bond investor does not need to wait a decade for all of their money to be returned because they receive a small portion of the money back in the form of interest payments. Duration calculates the average time it would take the investor to receive all of his money back on a bond investment. For a regular bond, the duration will always be less than its time to maturity. Even in a bond yielding 2 percent, its duration will be less than ten years, but it will be close. Duration tells you how much a bond's price is likely to rise or fall if interest rates change, and it can be used as a measurement of interest rate risk. The longer the duration, the higher the interest-rate risk.

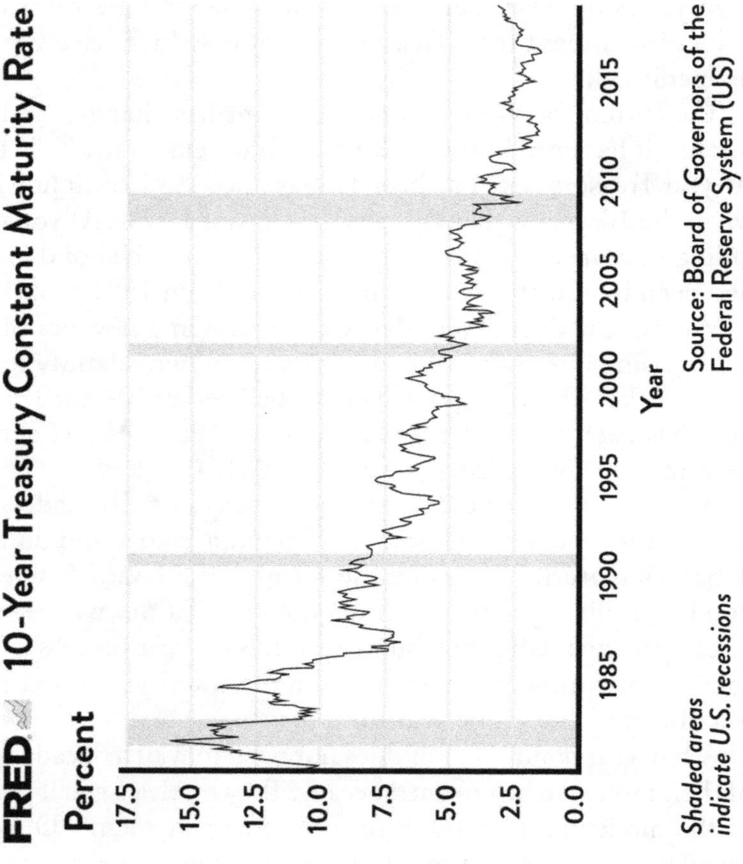

Figure 16.[75]

[75] Board of Governors of the Federal Reserve System (US), 10-Year Treasury Constant Maturity Rate [DGS10], retrieved from FRED, Federal Reserve Bank of St. Louis; https://fred.stlouisfed.org/series/DGS10, October 21, 2018.

The price performance of both stocks and bonds serves as a measure of economic activity, fueled by investors' perceptions of how well the market is doing. While you're most likely to see stock and bond performance reported in one, three, and five-year periods, it's best to view it over an entire market cycle and to be aware of your own personal investment time horizon, as that can have a large impact on your overall outcome.

A market cycle is the period between the two latest highs or lows of a common benchmark, such as the S&P 500.[76] A complete market cycle is a peak-to-peak period that contains a price decline of at least 20 percent from the previous market peak, followed by a rebound that establishes a new, higher peak.[77]

Predicting the direction of the stock market at any given time is very difficult, but not impossible. The stock market demonstrates well-defined and predictable cyclical patterns and trends. For example, there are a variety of event-driven cycles and patterns that are well-known, such as the presidential election cycle, which takes place every four years. Presidents like to have a strong economy around election time; if they must have a bad economy, they prefer it in the first year of their term, so the electorate will forget about it in the ensuing years.

The annual "Santa Claus Rally" is another relatively predictable cycle. Stocks often do well in December and early January, boosted by Christmas sales and large-scale corporate technology purchase. Companies often have lose-or-use tech budgets, and IT directors hate to see that money go unused. Another factor—people just seem cheerier around the New Year, and more inclined to buy

---

[76] "Market Cycles." Investopedia.com/terms/market cycles. Accessed 14 October 2018.

[77] Morgenson, Gretchen and Campbell R. Harvey. *The New York Times Dictionary of Money and Investing: The Essential A-Z Guide to the Language of the New Market.* Times Books, 2002.

stocks than sell them. You can see this effect year-round. Stocks usually rise the Friday before a holiday.

An investor who is knowledgeable and understands these cycles and patterns can optimize performance results. When used with the Adaptive Investment Portfolio, you can dramatically boost your ability to capture positive market returns through bull markets, bear markets, and everything in between, allowing your long-term investments to grow more quickly and more safely.

A good place to start is to understand whether the market is in a bull or bear posture. A bull market is defined by investor confidence, optimism, and rising prices. A bear market is a period marked by falling stock prices and low investor confidence. *The Wall Street Journal* and most financial media commentators commonly use 20 percent as a benchmark in uptrends and downtrends to identify the beginning of a new bull or bear market.

As you are undoubtedly aware, the current bull market in U.S. stocks, as measured by the S&P 500, became the longest in recent history on August 22, 2018, surpassing the bull market run that lasted most of the 1990s. Wall Street is in the business of measurement, and measured the conventional way, as long as the S&P 500 fails to decline at least 20 percent, this bull market is considered ongoing.

Some strategies may perform well in a bull market, while others may outperform in a bear market. As discussed in chapter 3, passive strategies, such as index funds, do well in bull markets, but they offer no protection in bear markets—they simply follow the index. Because there's no manager, the fund can't raise cash to buffer downturns. In 2000 and 2007, major bear market years, stock index funds, and ETFs got clobbered.

One way of preparing for market risk is through diversification, which is why many investors use mutual funds. If you own 100 stocks, the collapse of one stock won't hurt that much. But most stock funds won't protect you from a bear market. They pretty much claw everyone, albeit to varying degrees.

The problem with bear markets is that, by definition, most people don't see them coming. You can, however, take note of some events that make a bear market more likely. Think of them as yellow flags.

For example, when the Federal Reserve begins raising rates, that's a yellow flag. The Fed can raise rates for a long time before it affects stock prices, but sooner or later, rising rates take their toll on stock prices. When interest rates rise, bonds and bank CDs look more appealing to investors.

DEBT

Debt can be an important driver in the economy because it helps to create growth when it is used in productive ways. For example, productive debt can be used to create assets which will yield income that is sufficient to pay the principle and interest on the loan. The purchase of rental properties can provide income to service the debt and also provide an opportunity for appreciation. But when debt is created by consumption that is used to live beyond one's means, that is as we all know a very bad thing. In addition to a paving the way to insolvency, this type of debt creates a more ominous problem. When money is borrowed to pay for something now, that would otherwise require time in order to earn and save for that purchase, it pulls that consumption forward, creating economic growth at the time of consumption. Eventually, the future of where the consumption would have taken place is reached and the consumption that was pulled forward is gone, leaving a void where it would have otherwise been. At that point growth falls, creating an economic slowdown. With the feverish expansion of public and private debt, in combination with rising interest rates, we could have some tough sledding at some point in the not-too-distant future.

This is another yellow flag that has been waving for some time—the U.S. national debt, which now stands at $21.4 trillion, or 108 percent of GDP, according to the International Monetary Fund. While people debate the actual size of the debt—a good chunk of which is the Social Security Trust fund—the debt is growing fast. Ten years ago, just prior to the financial crisis, the debt was approximately $9.5 trillion and represented about 64 percent of GDP.

It's not just the U.S. on a borrowing spree. Global debt has hit another record high of $247 trillion in the first quarter of 2018, up $70 trillion over that last decade. That is equivalent to 382 percent of developed-world GDP. In addition, American corporations are highly indebted, and have been binging on debt over the past decade because of record low interest rates.

The massive amount of corporate debt presents a potential problem and could aggravate a downturn when interest rates rise. This is because the increase in the amount of money needed to service the debt from higher interest rates crowds out additional investments in people, factories, and production. In addition, the more leveraged companies are, the less resilient they are to shocks and economic turbulence, which makes companies vulnerable. An increase in interest rates means higher borrowing costs, which leads to lower profit margins. The Institute of International Finance (IFF) has released a sobering report about the current state of global debt, which included this excerpt:

> U.S. non-financial corporate debt hit a post-crisis high of

> 72% of GDP: At around $14.5 trillion in 2017, non-financial corporate sector debt was $810 billion higher than it was a year ago, with 60% of the rise stemming from new bank loan creation. At present, bond financing accounts for 43% of outstanding debt with an average maturity of 15 years vs. the average maturity of 2.1 years for U.S. business loans. This implies roughly around $3.8 trillion of loan repayment per year. Against this backdrop, rising interest rates will add pressure on corporations with large refinancing needs.[78]

There are multiple points that are highlighted in the IIF note, one of which is that all corporations added significantly more leverage since the Great Recession. These elevated levels of debt will make businesses vulnerable when the next recession strikes if borrowing costs spike because of rising rates. Institutional investors have rules in place that require them to start selling troubled bonds at the first signs of trouble. The problem is that buyers disappear quickly in a downturn, resulting in sharply lower prices. Removing the easy money could trigger the next default cycle.

The last two market crashes have corresponded with peaks in corporate debt to GDP ratio.[79] According to David Lipton, deputy managing director of the International Monetary fund (IMF), "The prolonged period of low central bank interest rates and rising debt in developed economies possess the greatest threat to financial markets in the medium term."

---

[78] Maudlin, John. "Yet Another Debt Crisis is Brewing." *Forbes*. 13 June 2018. https://www.forbes.com/sites/johnmauldin/2018/06/13/yet-another-debt-crisis-is-brewing/#2ba64d4bff57. Accessed 16 October 2018.

[79] Bloomberg for the period 12/1/1989- 7/1/2016, accessed 9/6/17. Crash 1 occurred from January, 2000 to February, 2003. Crash 2 occurred from November 2007 to March 2009. Real Gross Domestic Product (GDP) is the value of economic output adjusted for inflation. Corporate debt is issued by a corporation and sold to investors.

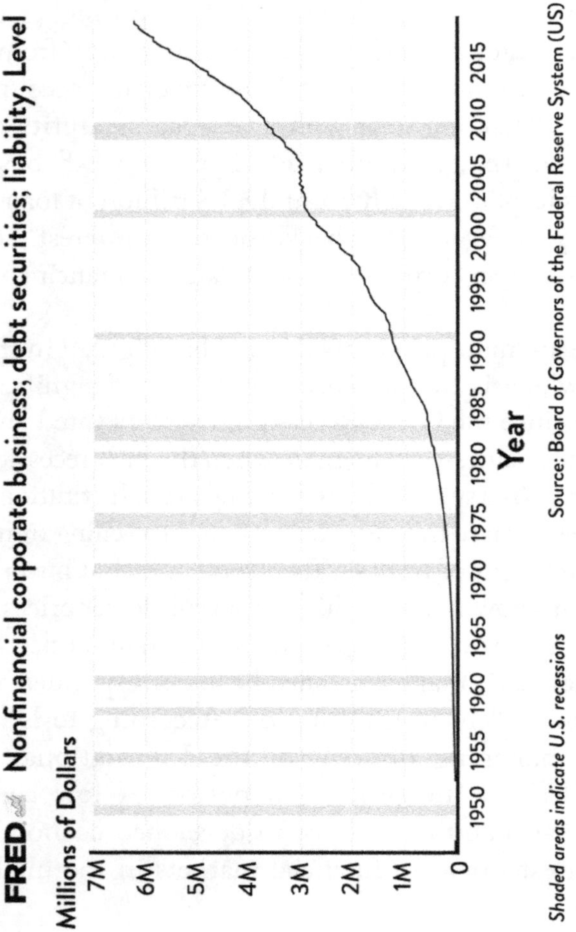

Figure 17.[80]

[80] Board of Governors of the Federal Reserve System (US), Nonfinancial corporate business; debt securities; liability, Level [NCBDBIQ027S], retrieved from FRED, Federal Reserve Bank of St. Louis; https://fred.stlouisfed.org/series/NCBDBIQ027S, October 24, 2018.

Lipton said that central banks' policy of buying bonds, implemented after the 2008 financial crisis to increase liquidity and encourage borrowing, now presents potentially harmful downsides. "In financial markets, there are risks that come from having low interest rates for a very long time," he said. "That's encouraging more risk-taking behavior, and its affecting the market risk that capital markets participants have."[81]

Furthermore, individuals and families have more debt burden than ever before. As interest rates increase, so does the payment on variable interest rate credit cards and home equity lines of credit. This can have a material negative effect on disposable income and consumption, contributing to a slow down and even defaults. This has a direct effect on housing, too. Rising rates typically slow the housing market as people buy house payments, not house price. Rising rates mean higher payments.

Greg Jensen, CIO at Bridgewater, the largest hedge fund in the world, is warning that 2019 is looking particularly dangerous, blaming the Fed's tightening. He noted, "Markets are already vulnerable, as the Fed is pulling back liquidity and raising rates, making cash scarcer and more attractive—reversing the easy liquidity and 0% cash rate that helped push money out of the risk curve over the course of the expansion. The danger to assets from the shift in liquidity and the building late-cycle dynamics is compounded by the fact that financial assets are pricing in a Goldilocks scenario of sustained strength, with little chance of either a slump or an overheating as the Fed continues its tightening cycle over the next year and a half."[82]

---

[81] Bercetche Joumanna and Natasha Turak. "Rising Debt and low interest posing greatest market risks, IMF's David Lipton says" *CNBC.* 15 November 2017. https://www.cnbc.com/2017/11/15/rising-debt-and-low-interest-posing-greatest-market-risks-imfs-david-lipton-says.html. Accessed 16 October 2018.

[82] Kern, Michael. "World's Largest Hedge Fund Claims Investors are in Danger." *Safehaven Preservation of Capital.* 5 June, 2018. https://safehaven.com/article/45570/Worlds-Largest-Hedge-Fund-Claims-Investors-Are-In-Danger. Accessed 16 October 2018.

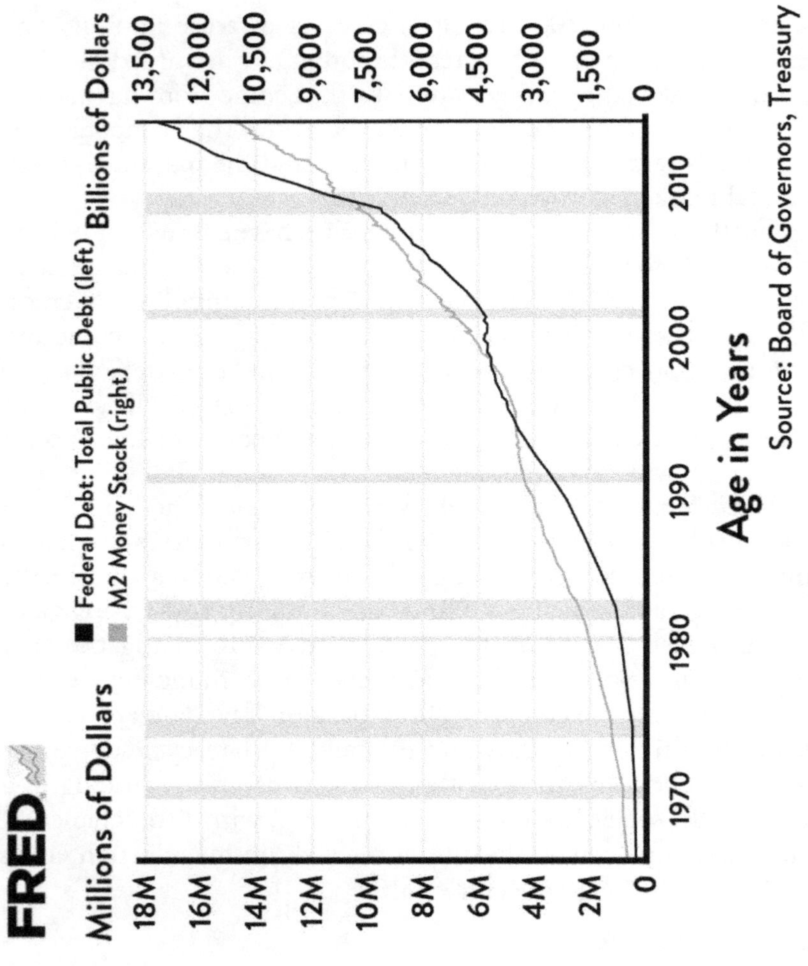

Figure 18.[83]

[83] Using quarterly returns for the period 1/1/1947 to 3/31/2017. Data source https://fred.stlouisfed.org. Accessed on 8/25/2017.

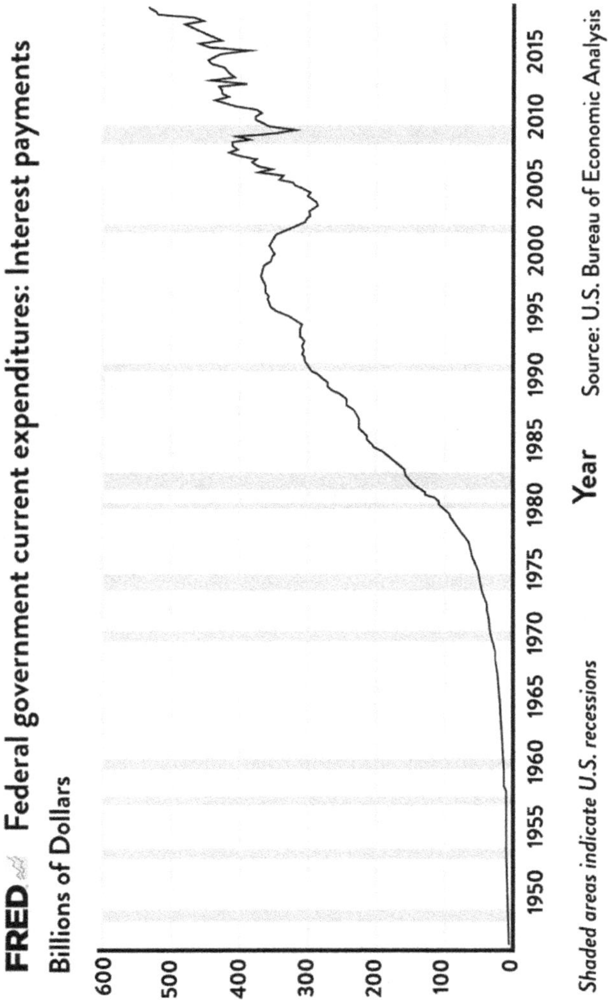

Figure 19.[84]

[84] U.S. Bureau of Economic Analysis, Federal government current expenditures: Interest payments [A091RC1Q027SBEA], retrieved from FRED, Federal Reserve Bank of St. Louis; https://fred.stlouisfed.org/series/A091RC1Q027SBEA, October 22, 2018.

WE ARE SPENDING MORE THAN WE ARE MAKING

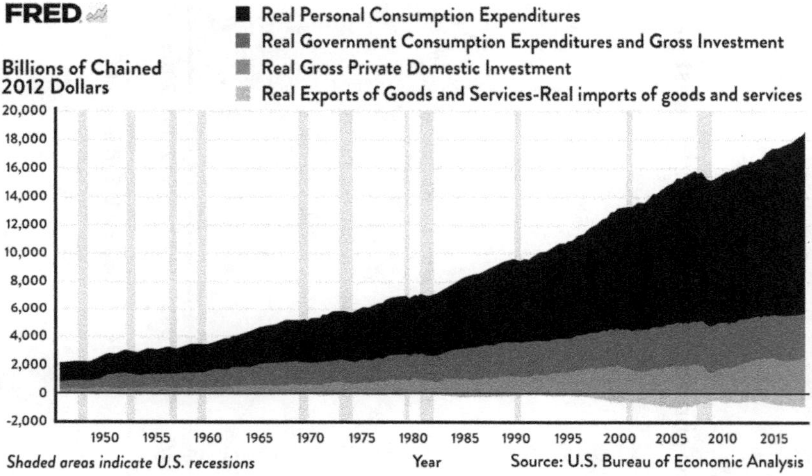

Figure 20.[85]

This is, of course, worrisome as the combination of record high levels of debt are on a collision course with rising interest rates. The obvious question becomes, given the massive amounts of debt in the world, how long can we all absorb higher rates without causing a serious market or economic event?

Debt and rising rates leave both stock and bond markets vulnerable. There has never been a time when the Federal Reserve has begun a rate hike cycle that did not eventually result in negative economic and financial market consequences. We have been in a

[85] U.S. Bureau of Economic Analysis, Real Personal Consumption Expenditures [PCECC96], retrieved from FRED, Federal Reserve Bank of St. Louis; https://fred.stlouisfed.org/series/PCECC96, October 22, 2018.

period of declining interest rates and debt expansion for thirty-five years. The end of that cycle can bring some real challenges—which is why portfolios need to be adaptive.

> *If I owe you a pound, I have a problem; but if I owe you a million, the problem is yours.*
>
> *John Maynard Keynes*

MARGIN DEBT

Not only are governments, corporations, and individuals engulfed in record levels of debt, many investors are also levered up in the form of margin debt—which is the practice of borrowing against brokerage accounts. Margin debt tends to increase alongside stock market rallies as portfolio managers seek to add to portfolio performance, and exuberant investors chase the good feelings and easy money that are indicative of a rising market.

Investors buy individual stocks in two types of accounts. They either buy stocks in a cash account where they pay for the securities in full and have a full equity or ownership position, or they buy stocks on margin. In a margin account, the investor puts up a percentage of the purchase price, and the brokerage firm puts up the balance. The money that the investor places into the account is the "equity" and the brokerages portion is called the "margin" or "debit balance," which is just another name for loan. The brokerage firm borrows the margin amount from a commercial bank at one rate and lends it to the client at a higher rate. The brokerage firm keeps the purchased stock as collateral for both of the loans, the one to the customer and the one from the bank.

The percentage amount that the client has to put up to buy stock on margin is determined by the Federal Reserve Board in its Regulation T. Although the Federal Reserve determines the amount and writes the regulation, it is the New York Stock Exchange and the Financial Industry Regulatory Authority (FINRA) who enforce it. As outlined in Regulation T of the Federal Reserve Board, the initial margin requirement for stocks is 50 percent. As an example, an investor who wants to purchase $10,000 worth of stock on margin is required to put 50 percent of that, or $5,000 into the account. The brokerage firm lends the investor the other $5,000.

As we all know, stock prices fluctuate up and down. When the price of a stock goes up from the purchase price, the investor who has acquired that position on margin has "excess equity," which is a greater equity position than the initial 50 percent requirement. While there is some room for the value of the stock to decline without consequence, the amount of equity in the margin account has a minimum required level of 25 percent of the total value of the securities in the margin account. If the stock declines to the point where the investor's equity is less than one-third of the debit balance that is required, then the investor will get a margin call—a demand by the broker for the investor to deposit additional money or securities into the account so that the account is brought back up to the minimum required maintenance margin.

There seems to be no fear currently in the market, not even a little. In fact, it appears investors no longer believe in market cycles, fundamentals, or prudent portfolio and cash management. According to FINRA, investor margin debt reached a new high of $669 billion in May 2018, which is up more than 33 percent since 2007. This dramatic increase has the potential to create significant market instability. This is because when the market goes down, which it always eventually does, many stock portfolios that are over-leveraged with margin debt are unable to cover their related margin requirements, resulting in margin calls. When that happens, brokers start the forced liquidation of customer accounts to cover the debt. This can send the market down sharply and indiscriminately. Does this remind you of 2006 when people were borrowing money against their houses to buy another house, or two?

As I have already mentioned, I am an optimist by nature but also a prudent realist. My job is to protect and grow clients' assets. The increasing levels of margin debt are not indicative of an imminent crash, but are flashing a warning sign. Investors should be aware and exercise caution and prudent risk management.

Keep in mind that the average bull market lasts only about four-and-a-half years, putting the current record setting bull market in territory never seen before. Of the twelve bull markets since World War II, only half have lasted five years, and only three have made it to six years. The current bull market recently celebrated its ninth birthday on Wednesday, August, 22, 2018, making it the longest in history with the greatest percentage gain for the Dow post-World War II, according to the Leuthold Group.

During the technology boom of the 1990s, stock prices started to accelerate late in the decade. Margin debt followed that rise, increasing into 1999 and peaking in March of 2000. That same month the S&P 500 hit its all-time daily high.

There was a similar surge in margin debt that began in 2006 and peaked in July 2007, just three months before the market peaked. A hallmark of these last two boom-and-bust cycles was leverage. On the way up, leverage is a wonderful thing, allowing for extended gains as the markets churn ever higher. However, as history clearly demonstrates, leverage is far more awe-inspiring in reverse as the unwinding of debt feeds on itself and the result is waterfall market declines.

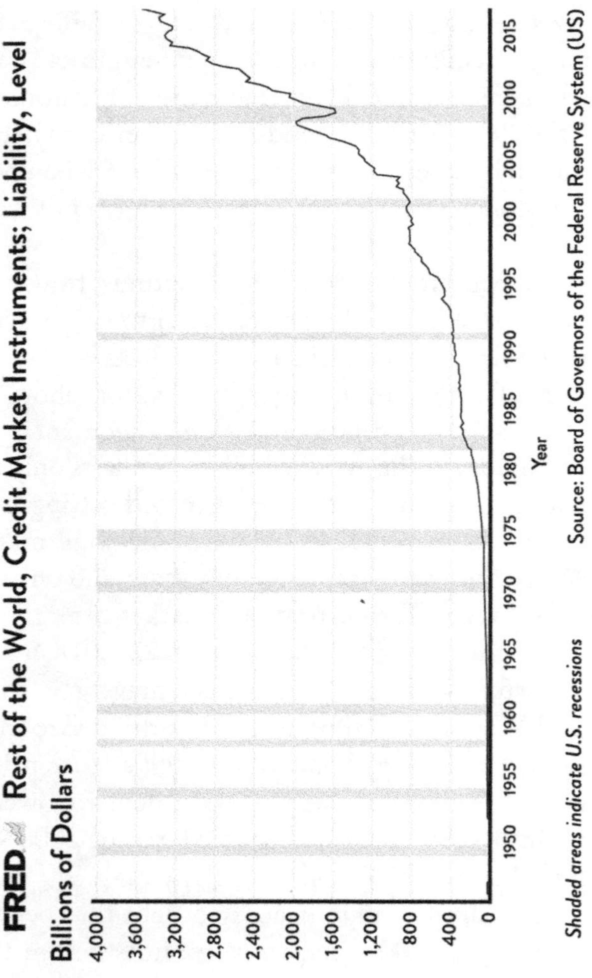

Figure 21.[86]

[86] Board of Governors of the Federal Reserve System (US), Rest of the World; Credit Market Instruments; Liability, Level [DODFFSWCMI], retrieved from FRED, Federal Reserve Bank of St. Louis; https://fred.stlouisfed.org/series/DODFFSWCMI, October 22, 2018.

FAT TAILS & BLACK SWANS

A black swan is an event or occurrence that deviates beyond what is normally expected of a situation and is extremely difficult to predict. Black swan events are typically random. The term is based on an ancient saying that people presumed black swans did not exist—until they were discovered in the wild. The saying was popularized by Nassim Nicholas Taleb after the financial crisis of 2008. Taleb argued that black swan events are impossible to predict, yet have catastrophic ramifications. Thus, it is important to always assume that black swan events are a possibility. Taleb's suggestion is not even to try predicting such random events, but to construct hedging strategies instead to protect against such events while simultaneously participating in positive events.[87]

Tail risk is a form of portfolio risk that arises when the possibility exists that an investment will move much more sharply than one could predict from its normal behavior. (The tail refers to either end of a bell curve). Traditional statistical analysis shows that 99.7 percent of all stock price variations fall within three standard deviations of the average; therefore, there is only a 0.3 percent chance of an extreme event occurring. A normal distribution assumes that, given enough observations, all values in a sample will be distributed equally above and below the average.

Many traditional models such as Modern Portfolio Theory and Efficient Market Hypothesis assume normality. In 1965 Eugene Fama published an analysis of the behavior of stock market prices that showed that they exhibited so-called fat tail distribution properties, which simply means that extreme movements were

[87] Taleb, Nassim Nicholas. *The Black Swan: The Impact of the Highly Improbable (2nd ed.)* Penguin, 2010.

more common than predicted.[88]

Fat tails are very difficult to foresee and, as a result, you should initiate a risk management strategy to protect a portfolio from unexpected events. Of course, insurance is only good if you have it before you need it. A properly designed portfolio will not only generate a good return by participating in an upward trend, but also will provide some protection against tail risk. This is an important component of the Adaptive Investment Portfolio. Creating a hedge or risk management strategy requires an active intention for minimizing downside participation.

---

[88] Fama, Eugene F. "The Behavior of Stock-Market Prices." *The Journal of Business*, vol. 38, no. 1, 1965, pp. 34-105. https://www.jstor.org/stable/2350752. Accessed 12 October 2018.

CHAPTER 7

WALL STREET MYTHOLOGY

Doubt is not a pleasant condition, but certainty is an absurd one.
- Voltaire

Big Wall Street firms have huge marketing machines and budgets to make sure you get their message loud and clear. While many start with a kernel of truth, they end up promising much more than can be delivered. After all, when something is repeated often enough, it can become widely accepted as truth. One of your jobs as an investor is to separate out the truth from the myths. Here are a few to be aware of.

MYTH ONE

In the long run, the stock market always goes up, so the buy-and-hold strategy is the only good investment strategy.

The Standard & Poor's 500 stock index has gained 10.22 percent annually since 1926, assuming you reinvested your dividends. Now that we are in the longest bull market ever, investors are beginning to forget history and are being lulled right where Wall Street would like them to be—all-in on bonds and long stocks, all of the time. (Going long means you're investing in the hope that prices will rise.) Investors are forgetting that there can be long periods of low or even no returns in the broader markets.

Memorialized by Peter Lynch, Warren Buffet, and Sir John Templeton,[89] the buy and hold approach is appealing to many investors. Lynch was the manager of Fidelity Magellan Fund and averaged a 29 percent return from 1977 through 1990. Warren Buffett, CEO of Berkshire Hathaway, has rolled up a $90 billion fortune in company stock. And John Templeton was a pioneer in global investing whose achievements gained him a knighthood. After all, if it's endorsed by these legends of finance, it must be true. All we need to do is simply put our money in an average stock mutual fund and let it sit there.

However, when we take a closer look at the history of each of these investors, a different picture emerges. For example, when Peter Lynch established his record as one of Wall Street's leading mutual fund managers, he held stocks less than one year on average.[90] It would be a real stretch to suggest that is "buy and hold." In fact, Lynch's average holding period for a stock was less than eight months; one year it was even less than four months.

Templeton, associated with globally diversified mutual funds and known as one of the great value investors, said, "All things cycle in and out of favor; investments and investment styles." The implication is obviously that one needs to be ready to change along with a change in the markets.

Warren Buffet does not subscribe to the Efficient Market

[89] Warren Buffett, Sir John Stapleton, Peter Lynch: How to invest like the financial gurus." *Financial Post.* https://business.financialpost.com/investing/warren-buffett-sir-john-templeton-peter-lynch-how-to-invest-like-the-financial-gurus. Accessed 16 October 2018.

[90] Source: Morningstar Principia

Hypothesis as a value investor, but nevertheless is declared the buy-and-hold king by the media. True, he once declared, "My favorite holding period is forever." However, upon closer inspection of Buffet's actions, this claim falls apart. It is clear that he will regularly move in and out of big positions. In fact, as the story goes, Buffet opened his first fund in 1956 with $105,000 when he was twenty-six years old. In just thirteen years the fund grew to $105 million in assets. Despite the success of the fund, Buffet became weary of the economic climate and Wall Street's future and shut down the firm in 1969.[91]

Furthermore, what people forget is that the 10.22 percent average rate overlooks vast fluctuations in value, and that much of your return depends on when you buy and sell. Had you bought the Vanguard 500 Stock Index Fund in March 2000—the eve of the tech wreck—you would have gained 5.93 percent a year through June of 2018, assuming you were able to resist the temptation to sell. Since 1960, the S&P 500's annualized ten-year gains have ranged from 17.55 to -2.22 percent. That's right—a negative number.

And if the best strategy was to buy and hold, then why do major Wall Street firms have proprietary trading desks? They are not holding for the long term, particularly when there are market disruptions. If that was in fact true, there would be no such thing as a professional hedge fund manager; there would be no need for a hedge at all. Furthermore, there would be no price volatility at all—market prices would be stable.

Hedge fund managers do not buy and hold. As we have come to learn, most investors simply don't do that either. Hedge fund managers will buy and sell in order to profit from market inefficiencies or on companies that are under or over-valued. Individual

---

[91] *Becoming Warren Buffet.* HBO, 2017

investors tend to sell in and out of funds driven by the emotions of fear and greed, and their timing is usually horrible.

It is important to distinguish who the clients and customers of large Wall Street firms are. The big Wall Street firms generate a large percentage of their revenue from their investment banking relationships with large corporations, governments, and wealthy individuals. The typical Wall Street firm raises capital for its clients by underwriting new securities, such as stocks and bonds. They may also assist their corporate clients with mergers and acquisitions, market making, and trading. These firms generate profit by charging fees and commissions for providing those services.

Wall Street needs its customers (you) to buy the products they created for their clients (not you). It would obviously be much less profitable and not in the best interest of their institutional clients if they were to tell you to "sell" when they need you to buy.

One of my first jobs as a teenager was in a restaurant where I started out busing tables and shortly thereafter became a waiter. It was during this time that I learned that the "chef's special" is not always really special at all. More often than not, the fish, rack of lamb or whatever the special may be is old and needs to be sold before it goes bad, at which point it becomes a loss.

In the restaurant business, this is known as spoilage, and it is a normal fact of life as produce, dairy, and meats have a limited shelf life. Although there are ways that restaurants avoid excessive spoilage, pushing items as "special" out the door is one of their tricks. As a for-profit business, this is standard operating procedure to protect the bottom line.

Similarly, investment banks protect their bottom line by selling investors the "specials" of the day, which need to get out the door before they spoil. Your interests and Wall Street's interests may not always be the same.

It is when the market seems to be only going up that we hear the four most dangerous words in investing: "This time is different." In every bubble, central bankers, policy makers, media wonks, and investors are fully convinced that the good times will never end. It's important to remember during periods such as these that the basics of economics do not really ever change—and neither does human behavior.

As an example, the recent bubble in the U.S. housing market continued to inflate despite a series of cautionary red flags. In 2005 and 2006, U.S. home price increases far outpaced growth in gross domestic product (GDP) and personal incomes. In retrospect, home prices were clearly in a speculative bubble. Yet, even as housing prices soared, former Federal Reserve Chairman Alan Greenspan argued that the economic situation was different this time around. He theorized that financial breakthroughs like widespread securitization made real estate more liquid and supported rising prices.

MYTH TWO

To be a successful investor, all you need to do is invest in a bunch of highly diversified, passively managed funds that mimic an index and stay the course.

While mutual funds have their place in an investor's portfolio, they are not the magical fix-all to the challenge that many investors face and even pose some unique risks. The main benefit of a mutual fund is diversification. If a number of stocks or a sector melts down, it's better to own 100 stocks than seven stocks. Don't put all your eggs in one basket. Large funds own hundreds of individual stocks. As highly diversified mutual fund strategies gain assets, inefficiencies become more prevalent because share prices are increasingly driven by factors other than fundamentals. Too many investment positions and over-diversification inhibits a fund manager's ability to fully understand the risks taken with each security, creating potentially greater risk. Further, owning too many stocks in a fund can dilute the benefits of a fund's best picks.

In *Modern Portfolio Theory and Investment Analysis*, by Edwin J. Elton and Marin J. Gruber, the authors conclude that the average standard deviation (risk) of a single stock portfolio was 49.2 percent. That's high. Increasing the number of stocks in the average well-balanced portfolio could reduce the portfolio's standard deviation to a maximum of 19.2 percent. In the study, they also found that in a portfolio of 20 stocks, the risk was reduced to 20 percent. However, increasing the number of stocks from 20 to 1,000 only had the effect of reducing the portfolio's risk by about 0.8 percent, while the first 20 stocks reduced the portfolio's risk by 29.2 percent. Warren Buffet said, "Wide diversification is only required when investors do not understand what they are doing."

Although mutual funds have positive attributes, they are just one incomplete part of an overall investment strategy. While they do provide investors with asset diversification, they do not provide a risk management strategy, which is critical to protecting us in down markets, and helps us to sleep at night when markets get choppy, as they always eventually do.

It is also important to understand a fund's treatment of taxes, as well as its fees. Some funds are highly tax-inefficient vehicles. When a fund sells a stock at a profit, it passes the taxable gain on to you. When a fund receives a dividend, it distributes that to you—and the tax liability as well. Most index funds don't pass much on in the way of capital gains, although they can pass on large dividend payouts.

And then there are the fees. Many broker-sold funds have a front-end sales charge as high as 5.75 percent, which means you start your investment program with a loss. All told, the effects of taxes, sales charges, and fees can take a hefty toll. Consider the Eaton Vance Income Fund of Boston. The $4.9 billion fund has gained an average 4.84 percent a year the past five years, using conventional reporting methods. Adjust for the fund's 4.75 percent sales charge and taxes, however, and its return shrinks to 1.29 percent annually.

The fund is geared towards income, which is taxed at your regular income tax rate. And its maximum sales charge is fairly common for most bond funds. But in addition to taxes and sales charges, the fund has an annual 1 percent expense ratio. What's that? Mutual funds are required to disclose how much they charge annually to run the fund, which they do as an annual percentage of assets. It's the cost of paying managers, printing prospectuses, and other expenses the fund might have.

MYTH THREE

Be patient. The market will bounce back.

Yes, it almost always has, but it can take a long time. The Dow Jones Industrial Average didn't recover from the Great Crash of 1929 for twenty-five years, and it did so with many different stocks than were in the index in 1929. On average, it has taken investors fourteen months to recover from a garden-variety bear—a loss of 20 percent to 39.9 percent—and 58 months to recover from a mega-bear—a loss of 40 percent or more. Recovery, incidentally, isn't guaranteed. The Japanese stock market has never topped its 1989 peak.

Finally, there's the remorseless mathematics of losses. Volatility may actually be more important to your portfolio's value than average annual returns. That's why downside protection is critical to helping you to stay on track toward your investment goals. You already knew that downward market volatility is a natural part of investing, but did you know what the long-term effects were on your overall portfolio? Managing risk matters!

Consider this: an individual decides to retire after a lifetime of hard work just as the market falls. A typical portfolio subject to market returns would therefore be negatively impacted, and the potential outsized effect could come as a shock. A mere loss of 10 percent would require an 11 percent gain to recover, which is quite manageable. However, as the loss grows, the size of the return needed to recover increases at a faster pace. For example, if you were to lose 50 percent, you would need to earn 100 percent gain to just to break even and recover your losses. With an annual return of 10 percent, that would take you more than seven years to recover. The more you lose, the greater the amount you must make to get your money back.

Think it can't happen? Think again. In 2008 when the Dow began its precipitous fall, ultimately losing about 54 percent, millions of would be retirees had to place their retirement plans on hold. Many investors had more concentrated, leveraged exposure and experienced even greater losses. With markets once again hitting fresh new all-time highs, pre-retirees seem all too eager to enjoy the cresting equity wave and forget the importance of downside risk protection. This is known as sequence-of-return risk and it can decimate hard-earned retirement plans. The catastrophe is something from which the retiree may never fully recover, diminishing the quality of life they have worked so long and hard for.

AMOUNT OF LOSS	RETURN REQUIRED TO BREAKEVEN	# OF YEARS TO BREAKEVEN WITH ANNUAL RETURN OF 10%*
- 10%	11.1%	1.1
-15%	17.7%	1.7
-20%	25.0%	2.3
-25%	33.3%	3.0
-30%	42.9%	3.7
-35%	53.9%	4.5
-40%	66.7%	5.4
-45%	81.8%	6.3
-50%	100.0%	7.3

Figure 22. *10% was chosen as a reference to the long-term annualized return of the S&P 500 Index. The chart above is hypothetical for illustrative purposes only.

There are many investors who fail to realize that it's not only the monetary loss, but also the loss of time in which to make the money back that have the potential to derail their future plans of retirement. This is not as much of an issue for younger people who do have time, but it is an issue for older people. Most investors do not start making enough money to start seriously saving and investing for their retirement until they are between 35 and 40 years old. That means that they really only have a few market cycles in order to reach their financial retirement goals. If they happen to catch a period where returns are flat for an extended period of time, or if that cycle happens to have a major crash, then the effects on their savings can be dramatically impaired as there are often long periods of time that the investors will need in order to get back to break even.

It is a well-documented fact that markets go through cycles, which include periods of time when stocks represent a dynamic opportunity for wealth creation and investors should be fully-invested. However, there are also periods of time during a normal cycle when market exposure and risk should be limited, thereby avoiding losses and even capitalizing on the downturn with short alternative or adaptive diversifier strategies. A passive buy-and-hold strategy relies a lot on chance and hope, and, as I often tell my two young sons, hope is not a strategy.

The great advantage of having a part of your investment portfolio actively managed is the avoidance of the major market corrections and crashes. By keeping a portion of your investments out of the market during these periods of market drawdowns, you prevent significant capital destruction, which not only preserves the principal, it also protects against the loss of time that it takes to recapture the loss—significant and important time that you invested in earning that capital.

With time and capital working in your favor, you then are presented with an opportunity to buy back into the market at much lower levels when market conditions have normalized. The Adaptive Investment Portfolio helps you manage risk and avoid major market events and puts you well ahead of where you would be had you simply employed a passive approach. The methodical and measured process of the Adaptive Investment Portfolio provides the structure to buy low and sell high, not buy high and sell low.

Being able to protect your investments by adapting to rapidly-changing market conditions can have dramatic effects on portfolio returns and your overall investment outcome, not to mention your peace of mind. In effect, the framework provides a self-disciplining mechanism to manage your own emotional behavioral biases, which are the biggest downfall for investors. You will have the peace of mind and staying power to meet your retirement and investment goals.

It is extremely important to consider your time horizon as it coincides with the market cycle, but there is another pitfall associated with bear markets called opportunity cost to watch out for as well. Investors often forget about opportunity cost, which is the loss of potential gain in investments you didn't make. It can be heart stopping to watch your portfolio get pummeled in a declining market.

Those who tell you that you cannot time the market are simply wrong. The truth is that you can. It is not an approach for the lazy advisor or inattentive home gamer. It takes hard work, rigorous analysis, and mental fortitude, but the astute investor can exploit market inefficiencies and benefit from them. The alternative is to have your money invested in what is essentially an assembly-line process that will assign you to one of two or three off-the-shelf, pre-built portfolios built for the masses.

MYTH FOUR

Passive investing is the only way to go.

Vanguard, the largest mutual fund company in the country, built its empire on the premise that index investing is superior to funds that are actively managed. But even Vanguard says that actively managed funds have a place in your portfolio—a good thing, since the Valley Forge, Pennsylvania, company offers dozens of actively-managed funds.

Vanguard believes—with good reason—that what crushes many active managers is the relatively high expenses they charge. It's hard enough to beat the S&P 500—doing so while subtracting 1.5 percent or even 2 percent a year is nearly impossible. "In short, we believe active management strategies do have a future, though we also believe that the relatively expensive active strategies of the past are likely to fall increasingly out of favor," the company stated.[92]

Dan Wiener, editor of the *Independent Adviser for Vanguard Investors*, has monitored the company for decades. His conclusion? "I'm not a buyer of mutual funds," he told *Kiplinger's Personal Finance* magazine. "I'm a buyer of managers. A good stock picker can outperform his or her index. It's easier to do that at Vanguard because Vanguard funds have low expense ratios, whether they are index funds or actively-managed funds."[93]

Not all active managers—even those whose funds are relatively inexpensive—are good managers. And not all good managers stay good. That's why it's important to choose managers carefully—and to keep an eye on performance at all times.

It can take a long time to get all the way back to the break-even point after you experience large drawdowns. The important takeaway here is that a proactive risk management strategy, along with the avoidance of large losses, can be more important than beating the market on the upside. That's what the Adaptive Portfolio offers.

---

[92] Vanguard. "Why Active Management has a Future." *ETF.com*. 16 July 2018. https://www.etf.com/sections/etf-industry-perspective/vanguard-why-active-management-has-future. Accessed 16 October 2018.

[93] Huang, Nellie S. "Why Vanguard's Actively Managed Funds Are a Better Bet." *Kiplinger's Personal Finance*. September 2014. https://www.kiplinger.com/article/investing/T041-C009-S002-dan-wiener-likes-vanguard-actively-managed-funds.html

CHAPTER 8

THE ADAPTIVE INVESTMENT PORTFOLIO

Intelligence is the ability to adapt to change.
- Stephen Hawking

It's October 2008, the market is already down nearly 20 percent, and news of the collapse of Lehman Brothers hits the wires. The S&P 500 tumbles another five percent that day, and the news is full of fears that a collapse of the entire financial system is imminent. Fearing the worst is yet to come, you decide to sell. You don't get back into the market until 2014—missing gains of 26 percent in 2009, 15 percent in 2010, two percent in 2011, 15 percent in 2012, and 32 percent in 2013. You've fallen victim to the biggest single obstacle in investment success: yourself. You gave in to your emotions when times were bad, and assumed that because the market was bad recently, it would always be that way.

We are currently in the longest bull market in history. America's economic expansion is old enough that people are now wondering what will cause the next cyclical downturn or bust. Left unchecked, behavioral tendencies in investing have been shown to have severe consequences for investor portfolios. Clearly, what you need is a way to protect yourself and remain disciplined in down markets and keep invested during bull markets.

And that's what the Adaptive Investment Portfolio seeks to do, by providing a disciplined, risk-controlled approach to investing. Rather than a bare-knuckled buy-and-hold *modus operandi*, the Adaptive Investment Portfolio uses a three-pronged strategy to keep you from being your own worst investment enemy, even in times of market and economic stress. You may have gotten the impression from previous chapters that you face an array of obstacles on your path to financial freedom, many of which look remarkably like you. While a stock market collapse and an economic downturn can surely steal your wealth, they can also create tremendous opportunities for wealth accumulation when navigated properly. It is how you react to a changing world that can help or hinder you most in your efforts to grow your wealth and secure your future. And that's where the Adaptive Investment Portfolio comes in.

We invest our hard-earned money to protect our families, improve our futures, and to have more free time. We invest to achieve our goals of buying a home, educating our children, and retiring comfortably. When markets turn nasty, our future and all our plans for it are threatened. We are all human and even though we don't mean to, we lose discipline, forget our time horizon, and with the best intention of protecting our futures, we make a fear-based decision.

Throughout the history of the stock market, investors have been conditioned to believe that the only way to participate in the growth of the stock market was to agonize through periods of market declines with a set allocation of stocks, bonds, and cash. While that approach is possible, most people simply don't have the emotional fortitude to lose tens of thousands, hundreds of thousands, or even millions of dollars and stay the course.

In fact, as seen in a recent study by Dalbar,[94] the investor who uses a basic allocation strategy has achieved only a little more than a third of the S&P 500's 14.5 percent annualized return since the current bull market began in March 2009. Blame it on the soul-searing bear market that preceded the current bull. The S&P 500 fell 44 percent from Oct. 9, 2007, through March 9, 2009. A loss of that magnitude requires a 79 percent gain just to break even. The Adaptive Investment Portfolio directly addresses those issues, allowing investors to stay the course, smoothing out the emotional ride, and therefore increasing the possibility of a positive outcome.

If you had relatives who lived through the Great Depression, you know that many retain a deep distrust of stocks (and banks). Big bear markets leave big scars. It's no wonder that people refer to the current market as one of the most hated bull markets ever. From Jan. 1, 2016, through July 31, 2018, the S&P 500 soared 45.23 percent with dividends reinvested. Yet investors yanked $202 billion from domestic stock funds and Exchange Traded Funds (ETFs), according to the Investment Company Institute, the fund industry's trade association.

Since 2009, the stock market has experienced seventeen pullbacks of five percent or more. With the financial crisis still fresh in their minds, investors were pessimistic and emotional at the beginning of 2009 and underinvested in stocks. They were waiting for the next downturn to occur and hesitant to get back into the market. As the market conditions improved, investors started to re-enter the market again, only to get shaken out as soon as a market had even a small downturn—that is why most allocation investors have only experienced a 5.1 percent return since the

[94] "Qualitative Analysis of Investor Behavior." *Dalbar*. 2018. https://www.dalbar.com/QAIB. Accessed 17 October 2018.

bull market began.

What is currently taking place is an example of recency bias, which we discussed in chapter two. It can occur from a consistently strong market expansion, such as the one we have recently experienced, but the Great Recession has left a long shadow. Despite enormous returns since 2009, many investors have missed most of this massive bull market. Now, unfortunately, they may be getting onboard too late, because investors evaluate their opportunities based in the most recent stock performance, regardless of what financial conditions and data are signaling ahead. The biggest drag on investor performance over time is allowing emotions to dictate investment decisions.

Part of the process of creating a successful portfolio is to prepare investors for changing global markets and for the unexpected, the Adaptive Investment Portfolio does just that. Most asset allocation models are focused on an outdated buy-and-hold investment approach that is not able to adapt to an ever-changing and increasingly dynamic global investment landscape. The Adaptive Investment Portfolio is a dynamic, three-mandate process that allows you to have confidence in all market environments.

Before we get into details, it's important to remember that the Adaptive Investment Portfolio is personalized to your risk tolerance, your financial goals, your time horizon, and to other financial considerations such as income and total assets. I get all of that information the old-fashioned way: by talking about them and by talking about you. (And there's also the risk tolerance quiz, discussed earlier.) Once we've figured out your needs and your risk tolerance, we create a personal investment policy statement, which provides the guidelines of how we invest your money in the Adaptive Investment Portfolio.

INVESTMENT POLICY STATEMENT

I had a dinner meeting with a prospective new client—let's call him Steve—at trendy new spot in Beverly Hills. Steve is educated, smart, and self-made. As we had dinner, discussing travel, family, and his financial goals, the conversation evolved to long-term planning and the performance of his current portfolio. I asked him about his Investment Policy Statement (IPS), and Steve gave me a quizzical look and asked, "What?"

Surprisingly, Steve is not the first high net-worth investor who has responded to my question about an investment policy statement this way. Like many other savvy investors, Steve said the goal was obvious, "To make money."

I responded, "That's true, but not always so simple. I was taught at an early age that if I have a goal or something to do and it is not written down, then it is not clear." Writing things down provides not just clarity, but also something concrete in order to gauge your direction and progress.

I explained that an Investment Policy Statement defines your portfolio's objectives, as well as its risk/reward parameters. For example, you might want to plan for your child's college education and your retirement. Both will probably have a different time frame. Your kids might go to college in ten years, and you might want to retire in twenty years. You can take more risk with a twenty-year time horizon than you can with a ten-year time frame, because you have more time to make up for down markets. The IPS document guides all future investment decisions and forms a central repository for all intelligence regarding investment decisions, objectives, and tax sensitivities.

The IPS makes clear why you are investing and how you will do so in order to best achieve those goals. It will include the types of investments the family will use, and what they will avoid. It will also define a family's maximum "capital risk"—the maximum drawdown of an investment they are willing to accept. It also establishes a clear plan of action for bullish and bearish market cycles, which helps to provide peace of mind during market fluctuations. Getting clear on the objectives gets everyone rowing in the same direction.

Excellent advice and thoughtful planning for all outcomes that can affect a family can be life-changing, and help to ensure a good outcome for the current and future generations, while a lack thereof can have devastating effects. I recall a young man to whom I was introduced in late 2017. As a young boy, he had inherited a $50 million fortune that was left to him by his father, a titan of corporate America. From the time he inherited that fortune to the time I had met him, he had lost over $18 million: more than a third of its total.

This was extremely disturbing to me. As an investment professional, I saw that the most glaring problem was that we were deep in the throes of a raging bull market and virtually all assets were experiencing dramatic price appreciation. Stocks, bonds, real estate, art, and collectible cars were all appreciating widely. Sure, he still had an enormous amount of money, but I could not fathom what could have gone so terribly wrong that this young man had experienced a loss of over 36 percent during that time. How was that possible?

I began to review his account statements and started identifying problems immediately. To begin with, his account had only 31 percent allocated to stocks. A basic rule of thumb that can help simplify the complexities of asset allocation is that stocks in a portfolio should be equal to 100 minus the investor's age. So for this young man in his early twenties, his equity allocation should have been at or near 80 percent. Another 50 percent of his portfolio was in hedging strategies.

He did take a monthly distribution through his trust, but that was nominal and reasonable for the amount of wealth he had. Over the time he had experienced those biblical losses, the S&P 500 had returned a total of over 85 percent, which should have launched his account to nearly $130 million. I was saddened by the enormity of the loss of capital, especially by the human side of the story. As this young man came of age and first learned about the mistreatment of his inheritance, he started to lose trust in people. He felt personally mistreated—not just by the people who were responsible for the stewardship of his estate, but by people in general. After all, his father had an amazing career and was able to leave a meaningful estate to his son, one he worked his whole entire life to accumulate. If properly managed, it should have cared for generations of his family to come.

There is more to the story, as situations like this one tend to be very complicated. Do you remember the section in chapter 4 on who the real clients of the big Wall Street firms are? The investment firm and the trust company that held and managed the accounts are two of the largest and best-known in the world. What I can say is that his best interests were not looked after or protected, and it is a terrible shame.

Obviously, at such a young age this young man had no understanding or control of how this situation was handled. While there was more going on in this particular situation that resulted in an epic failure, it does shed light on the importance of an Investment Policy statement as an instrument designed to provide guidance on portfolio construction and direction. By design the ongoing review and management stipulated by the IPS will almost immediately detect when the mandate is off course. An IPS should have been in place on behalf of this young man, allowing him the benefits of a clearly-defined and focused mandate that would avoid deviations due to changing market conditions or fiduciary malpractice. Remember, if it is not written down, it is not clear.

THE ADAPTIVE INVESTMENT PORTFOLIO: AN OVERVIEW

When I was a young boy, I was in the garage with my grandfather, Walter, cutting some wood to repair some decking in the backyard. He is one of the few surviving World War II veterans, a farmer from Minnesota—a hard-working man with a big heart. He is one of those guys who does not say a lot, but when he does it is a gem of wisdom. (His brother, Augie, also fought in the war as a pilot. He and his crew were actually shot down in a raid over Ploesti, Romania, hub of the Axis oil supply. He was awarded a posthumous Purple Heart for his service and sacrifice, and the United States flag that was presented to our family hangs in my home.)

Anyway, when we were in the garage working to repair the deck, my grandfather asked me to cut a piece of wood that we would use to replace an older, rotted-out piece. I placed the wood on his workbench and used two separate vice grips to secure it so that I could cut it. I felt really good about the work I was doing. I wanted to impress my grandfather with my ability to work hard and complete the job.

I began to apply pressure to the saw and into the wood as I pushed the blade back and forth. The saw got caught a few times, so I pushed harder, but it still was not moving as smoothly through the wood as I had hoped.

I felt my grandfather watching me, and saw him smile a little as I struggled, until he finally came in closer to me and gave me a very simple lesson on how to use the saw properly. In this instance, we were cutting across the grain of the wood. We were using the correct crosscut saw, but I wasn't using it the right way. My grandfather showed me that the cut should be started with the teeth of the saw nearest the handle. He said, "Make a few back cuts with a pulling stroke until you get a nice opening in the wood. After the groove is started, a few short strokes will deepen the cut. Then push the saw with an easy, free running motion. That way you will be able to push easily, letting the saw blade do the work instead of trying to force it with your muscles."

It was a great afternoon with my grandfather. The lesson about letting the saw blade do the work was a simple one, but it has always stayed with me. Just like the saw, the Adaptive Investment Portfolio (AIP) is designed to do the work for you so you don't have to power through on your own. When constructed properly, the AIP should give the investor the peace of mind and confidence through any market cycle, up or down, letting the portfolio do the work.

The heart of the Adaptive Investment Portfolio itself is its three-dimensional strategy, a dynamic approach that assumes best-case market scenarios will happen. But it also provides protection against the possibility that worst-case scenarios could happen—we just don't know when. Each of the three parts of the portfolio—called mandates—are diversified across asset classes, investment styles, and investment managers. It is a common-sense approach that provides a disciplined methodology to avoid the tendency to buy high and sell low.

The Adaptive Investment Portfolio has the potential to deliver consistent risk-adjusted performance for your investment portfolio in any market environment because it contains growth strategies for bull markets along with the defensive capabilities and risk mitigation strategies for bear markets. This smooths out volatility, providing peace of mind (I call it a nerve-calming mechanism), which is critical in helping you stay committed through varying market cycles with grace and ease. Because the Adaptive Investment Portfolio has a diversified strategy that's designed for the unexpected, you'll have the *conviction* and emotional fortitude to stay the course.

A deep-dive analysis of each fund strategist, as well as the fund objective, is a key factor in the construction of the AIP. In the due diligence process that I employ during the selection of strategists, each must undergo a rigorous review to be considered for inclusion in the portfolio. I conduct an internal review in addition to the review that is conducted for my firm by an independent, institutionally focused consulting firm. This approach provides us with additional outside research and a proactive, objective view during the selection and qualifying process of a strategist under consideration. The evaluation process and ongoing monitoring of each strategist includes a number of factors, including the following:

1. **People**: Who is managing the money? What is their experience and their track record?
2. **Underlying investments**: A fund can have a great record because of one great pick. That's great, but we'd like to see a history of consistent overall performance, not just one lucky guess.
3. **Operations and compliance**: You never want to see something go wrong in the back office. And that includes legal and audit procedures, as well as disaster recovery procedures.
4. **Relevance to mandates**: We always go back to the Adaptive Investment Portfolio. A manager could be terrific, but if his

fund doesn't fit our purposes or your risk tolerance, we won't use him.

The nature of the Adaptive Investment Portfolio is that it's flexible. And that's why we have an ongoing monitoring process. That means not only measuring performance, but making sure that we understand it—both through portfolio analysis and through conversations with fund strategists.

Once we have fully vetted each strategist and their investment tactics, we further analyze those systems for their risk characteristics and assign them a numerical value, using the same scale of 1-100 that we use to identify the risk tolerance of each individual investor. This disciplined methodology provides the framework for a highly personalized result in the portfolio construction process. The blend of strategies across the board provides micro-tuning that can be seen as equivalent to how a stereo equalizer would be tuned for optimal sound. Similarly, the tuning of higher risk-score strategies with lower risk-score strategies results in a portfolio that is perfectly risk-adjusted to each individual. Portfolios can then be put into place with the complete confidence that the evaluation process in choosing from the best management firms in the world was used to determine and ensure the best allocations for each individual.

The following chapters will focus on each of the AIP's three mandates—the Strategic, the Tactical Mandate, and the Hedging or Risk-Diversifier Mandate.

CHAPTER 9

THE STRATEGIC MANDATE

Hope is not a strategy.
- Vince Lombardi

In military terms, strategy refers to the big-picture moves that define a campaign—its long-term goals and objectives. Tactics are specific operations that are used to achieve those strategic aims. In the Civil War, for example, the Union's strategy was to starve the South by using a naval blockade to keep them from getting supplies. Obviously, the Confederacy's strategy was to break the blockade. The use of the ironclad warship Merrimac in the Battle of Hampton Roads was a tactical move by the Confederates to accomplish their strategy.

In financial terms, strategic investments mean long-term investments and asset allocations that suit your goals, risk tolerance, and time frame. The Strategic Mandate is optimized to produce the expected return in the given global market environment. Managers selected for this mandate utilize the MPT-style of investment portfolio construction, trying to find the best tradeoff between risk and reward.

The Strategic Mandate allocation is typically the largest part of the Adaptive Investment Portfolio and can occupy 50 percent or more of a total portfolio, depending on the individual. It's a top-down approach, meaning it's based on our analysis of the global economic and financial landscape. We typically use passive investments—index funds and exchange-traded funds—in the strategic sleeve. It's designed to stay fully invested, and it seeks to capture and fully participate in total market returns by mimicking the overall market, providing wide exposure to moves up and down.

The risk and reward of this mandate depend on market direction. The mandate can invest in mutual funds, ETFs, and employ other strategies that include traditional stock, bond, and cash allocations. The investment approach in this mandate begins with understanding the fundamental pricing of not only the markets, but also of each of the sectors within the equity markets. That means identifying areas of the equity market to emphasize or avoid in structuring portfolio holding.

Within the bond markets, we use strategies that seek to determine the appropriate amount of credit risk and the amount of interest-rate risk that you should take. Properly structuring the bond assets within a balanced portfolio can at times be as important as managing the risk of equity holdings.

Current factors and environmental conditions can enter into the decision-making process to either reduce the potential impact of negative event risks, or to take advantage of abnormally depressed sectors of the market. These considerations include the following.

1. **Potential legislation and litigation**: Politics and investing don't usually mix. People predicted the world would end when George W. Bush was elected president, and they did the same when Barack Obama was elected. Both views were wrong. Nevertheless, if an industry undergoes a transformation

because of new legislation, you have to take that into account.

2. **Regulatory reform**: The banking industry perennially complains that it's overregulated, despite its storied history in wrecking the economy. When regulators ease their grip on banks, their stocks do, indeed rise. What happens later is another story.
3. **Macroeconomic conditions**: Greece is a tiny country in terms of its gross domestic product, but its debt crisis brought most of Europe's stock markets to their knees. The things that happen in world economy can affect everyone. Similarly, trade wars and tariffs can have a big effect on markets, and you have to make sure you understand all that's going on in the world when you invest.

Let's consider a hypothetical Strategic Mandate for a fifty-year-old single woman with a $3 million portfolio. She scored a 70 on her risk assessment, making her moderately aggressive. She plans to retire at sixty-five. She's healthy and can expect to live at least thirty more years, to age ninety-five.

In this case, the Strategic Mandate will be 60 percent of her portfolio, or $1.8 million. We could divide it, simply, this way:

- U.S. stocks: 50 percent, varying between 45 and 55 percent, depending on market conditions.
- International stocks: 20 percent, varying between 15 and 25 percent.
- Bonds: 20 percent, again varying between 15 and 25 percent.
- Cash: 10 percent, with a five percent allocation up or down.

Those allocations can shift, of course, if—for example—our entirely fictional client decides she wants to retire early or buy a vacation home. But at the outset, this is what the Strategic Mandate of her portfolio might look like. Over the past twenty years, this blend would have earned 7.72 percent from U.S. stocks, 5.43 percent from international stocks, 4.2 percent from bonds, and 1.9 percent for money market funds. Total return is about 6 percent.

Using passive investments in this sleeve can create considerable savings for our client. A typical actively-managed stock fund that Morningstar classifies as large-company blend, for example, often charges as much as one percent in fees each year—and, as we've seen, those fees can be considerably higher if the fund carries a sales charge, or load. Let's say the fund's gross performance equals the S&P 500—7.72 percent a year. Subtract a full percent a year, and that's 6.72 percent per year.

If we put $500,000 into that passively-managed fund with a one percent annual fee, it reduces our client's return from 7.72 percent a year to 6.72 percent. Over the course of twenty years, the fund will cost our investor nearly $7,530 for every $10,000 invested. (Here's the math: $10,000 invested at $7.72 percent for twenty years is $44,251.39. At 6.72 percent, it's $36,721.15.)

This is a highly simplified version of the Strategic Mandate. The equity portion, for example, could have exposure to small-company stocks, mid-cap stocks, and even emerging markets stocks, depending on your tolerance for risk and your goals. Nevertheless, the strategic mandate will be the largest portion of your portfolio. The next two mandates, the Tactical and the Hedging or Diversifier mandate, are typically smaller—but extremely important. We'll explore those in the next chapter.

CHAPTER 10

THE TACTICAL MANDATE

Strategy without tactics is the slowest route to victory. Tactics without strategy is the noise before defeat.
- Sun Tzu

Sun Tzu was a Chinese general who lived from 544 B.C. to 496 B.C., although there is much debate over his life and career. His book, *The Art of War*, became popular with American military leaders after World War II and is currently listed in the Marine Corps Professional Reading Program. In recent years, it has become a minor cult classic for business majors. Go figure.

Nevertheless, the point of the quote is this: an investment portfolio is guided by an overall plan, which we described in the previous chapter. The Strategic Mandate is the main component of the Adaptive Investment Portfolio. The Tactical Mandate is designed to take advantage of opportunities as they occur, and to defend gains against losses when they look likely.

In finance, tactical investing refers to a more flexible or active approach to choosing investments. Using such an approach, the fund strategist can quickly change a portfolio's risk profile and actively allocate capital from being 100 percent invested in equities to 100 percent allocated to cash, depending on the strategist's market outlook. In the Adaptive Investment Portfolio, we manage this mandate to pursue shorter-term, trend-following opportunities.

For example, Wall Street regularly has favorite sectors—technology one year, utilities another. Following these trends—and selling them when they peak—can be a rewarding short-term investment technique.

The asset managers and fund strategies we select for this mandate are a balanced complement to the investment characteristics of the strategic mandate. The tactical mandate is designed to insulate investors from the unpredictability of market cycles and to protect them from their own behavioral biases. Rather than taking a static approach by choosing a passive or active investment approach, the Tactical Mandate is dynamic and can move between the two approaches and automatically adjust investment positions to accommodate for changing economic conditions, market volatility, and market cycles.

Why do you need a tactical approach? Because you need part of your portfolio to shield you against market downturns. Active management creates an opportunity for a portfolio to outperform passive strategies alone and market benchmarks by taking advantage of market inefficiencies. While the markets often are mystifying on a day-to-day basis, they often have broad trends that you can follow. Taking advantage of these trends can add performance to your nest egg.

And that's important—not only because increasing returns is a good thing, but because reducing the gut-wrenching ups and downs of the market is a good thing, too. You're far more likely to follow an investment plan if you don't start sobbing every time you see a stock ticker. The typical buy-and-hold approach of simply diversifying among a broad number of stocks was a bust for many investors during the market crashes of 2000 – 2002 and 2007 – 2008. The overall market performance during that time showed that well-diversified mutual fund models could not prevent serious drawdowns in a nasty market. Many investors panicked and sold at or near the bottom.

Over time—weeks and months, or even years—stocks often follow trends. They don't call it the herd on the Street for nothing. In order to ride those trends, you have to learn how to identify them. One way to do so is through technical analysis, which is simply tracing trends through the most direct means possible—securities prices themselves. Technical analysis is the interpretation of the price action of an individual stock, commodity, futures contract, or any other tradable financial instrument as they are represented in various charts and patterns. A study of the charts and other statistical indicators can be used to determine price support, resistance, as well as a trading range and trend. This data can be important in identifying historically relevant price patterns used to forecast the potential directions of an individual stock or the overall market. Market patterns and trends tend to repeat themselves, which is why they are studied so closely. While markets change, companies come and go, and technology continues to make rapid advancements, as was pointed out by Jesse Livermore, human behavior and biases remain the same over time.

Every second of every day, hundreds of thousands of investors are bidding some stocks up and other stocks down. The same is true for bonds, cattle futures, and multitudes of other investments. These buy, sell (also known as the bid, ask) prices combined represent the best estimate of what a particular security is worth. As we noted in our section on Modern Portfolio Theory, many academics think that trying to outsmart the crowd is difficult indeed.

Finance professor Jack Treynor was the editor of the CFA Institute's *Financial Analysts Journal* and a co-founder of Modern

Portfolio Theory. Treynor believed that while individuals can be wildly wrong about stock prices, hundreds of individuals can often be surprisingly accurate. To prove his point, Treynor brought a jar filled with 810 beans to his investment classes, and invited students to guess how many beans were in the jar. The mean estimate was 841, although only two guesses were right. "Apparently, it doesn't take knowledge of beans, jars, or packing factors for a group of students to make an accurate estimate of the number of beans in a jar," Treynor wrote. "All it takes is independence."[95]

To a technical analyst, price movements can tell a story about the overall trends in securities. For example, a reasonable question might be whether or not technology stocks are in a bull or bear market. A relatively simple way to answer the question is to average the price of a technology index, smoothing out its daily gyrations. For example, an analyst might average the previous fifty days' prices. Each day, the analyst would drop the oldest price and add the newest, creating what's called a moving average. If the current price is above the fifty-day average, we get an indication that tech stocks are in an uptrend. Similarly, if the price falls below its average, the trend is running out of steam. More sophisticated analysis can use different time periods, or look at the rate of change of an average or an index.

This type of technical analysis can be used to detect trends below the surface of the broad market: whether large-company stocks or small-company stocks are trending upwards, for example, and which is rising the fastest. It can tell which industries are faring better than others, and which investment styles—growth or value, for example—are producing superior returns. Armed with that knowledge, we can tilt the Tactical Mandate to take advantage

[95] Treynor, Jack I. "Market Efficiency and the Bean Jar Experiment," *Financial Analysts Journal*, vol. 43, no. 3, 1987, pp. 50-53. https://www.jstor.org/stable/4479031. Accessed 14 October 2018.

of those trends.

Other indicators can give an idea of the overall strength of a rally. The advance/decline line, for example, starts at a random number: say, 100. The analyst then takes the number of stocks that have fallen in price that day from the number of stocks that have risen. A rising line indicates that more stocks are rising than falling, which is good. When the line turns down—and it often does so before a market decline—it means that a rally is weakening or being held up by just a few strong members of the stock index. (Technicians call this "market breadth.") A broad rally is always better than a narrow one, but if you can identify the stocks that are rallying, you can have a tactical edge.

You can use tactical strategies in bond markets, too. For example, consider high-yield bonds, more commonly known as junk bonds. While these bonds aren't the equivalent of lending to your deadbeat brother-in-law, they do have a higher risk of default than Treasury bills, bonds, and notes, which are backed by the full faith—and taxing power—of the U.S. government. A technician can look at the difference in yield between, say, 10-year Treasury notes and low-rated corporate bonds. When the spread is narrow—say, three percentage points—then junk bonds are probably overpriced. When the spread is very large—seven percentage points or more—then junk bonds are probably a bargain.

Tactical moves don't have to depend on technical analysis, although there is usually a component of technical analysis in most tactical strategies. Let's consider the bond market once again. Unlike stocks, bond prices tend to move up or down at a slower pace, so identifying and acting upon up or down trends can be more effective. Suppose, when looking at the 10-year Treasury note, we see a trend of steadily rising yields (which we do now, the 10 year Treasury just hit 3.25 percent). Pushing those yields higher are rising inflation, low unemployment, and a hawkish Federal Reserve board. (Fed presidents who want to raise rates are hawks; those who want to cut rates are doves.)

A fixed portfolio would simply hold a big, diversified bond fund and be done with, which could be a big mistake. Long-term bonds could lose a considerable part of their value in the coming years if yields continue to climb. The Tactical Mandate, however, might shift to short-term bonds, which feel less pain than long-term bonds when interest rates rise. Another path the Tactical Mandate may explore, is to build a bond portfolio that considers high-yield, emerging markets, floating rate, municipals, and preferred stocks.[96] As covered in chapter 2, credit risk rather than interest-rate risk, is a bigger driver of total return for these types of assets. The higher yields and lower correlations of these broad asset classes may provide an opportunity to construct a stronger, more adaptive portfolio. The Tactical Mandate might even increase cash holdings, such as money market funds and bank CDs, because when short-term rates rise, rates on those investments rises, too.

Other strategies can help guard against undue risk, as well. While there are many, here are a few examples:

> **Global equity hedge**: A hedged investment simply means that it includes a way to shield against market downturns. A classic hedge-fund strategy would make bets that certain stocks or sectors would rise, while making simultaneous bets that certain stocks or sectors will fall. Because this is a global strategy, it would have more opportunities to make

---

[96] Preferred stock is a type of stock which may have any combination of features not possessed by common stock, including properties of both an equity and debt instrument, and is generally considered a hybrid instrument.

investments than one that simply invested in U.S. securities. That is because American stock markets only count for about 50 percent of the world's stocks.

Long-short equity funds: These are funds that concentrate on stocks, but typically include bets on sectors that will fall. They can make those bets by shorting stocks—borrowing stocks from a brokerage, selling them, and hoping they can buy them back at a lower price. They can also use options and futures to make their bear bets. The balance of short to long positions will depend on the fund's macro outlook. I should note that finding a good long-short fund isn't always easy. Some stock pickers are great on the long side, and others are good on the short side. Finding a team that's good in both directions is rare.

Boston Partners Long/Short Research, an institutional fund, is the largest long-short fund around. It has $6.7 billion in assets, which represents a great deal of faith in the fund by large investors. While it gets four Morningstar stars, the fund, at this writing, has lost 2.18 percent in 2018 through August at a time when the S&P 500 has gained 9.94 percent. (And now, a quick word from our legal department: any fund mentioned in this book is for illustrative purposes only, and does not represent a recommendation to buy or sell.)

Long-short funds aren't only for stocks. You can also buy long-short bond funds, which can short Treasuries or corporate bonds as well as buy them. Many long-short funds, both stocks and bonds, can venture abroad as well. Other tactical strategies may include the following:

Tactical Income: This is a go-anywhere approach for income investors, meaning it can seek income from stock dividends, bonds, or cash, depending on current market conditions.

Active Tactical: These fund managers typically use a number of different tactical strategies, ranging from contrarian trading of S&P 500 indexes to seasonal trading patterns. For example, technical resistance levels, moving averages, price trends, mean-reversion patterns and fundamental macroeconomic factors may be utilized in this strategy. This analysis is used to determine which specific areas of the equity market to emphasize or avoid in structuring an equity portfolio.

Emerging markets: Emerging markets, such as Brazil or China, can offer spectacular gains—at the right times. They can also offer spectacular losses at the wrong time. Unless you're deeply steeped in the economy and stock markets of, say, Turkey, you're nearly always better off with a diversified emerging markets fund than a single-country fund. At this writing, for example, Qatar's stock market is up 14.3 percent, while Turkey is down 45.6 percent.

Sector rotation funds: Through late September 2018, the average healthcare fund has gained 18.93 percent, according to Morningstar, while the average gold fund has swooned 22.56 percent. A sector rotation fund simply looks for the sectors with the strongest momentum, on the assumption that stocks in motion, like objects in motion, tend to keep moving. Typically, these funds will concentrate in the top two or three sectors, moving in an out according to their relative strength to the S&P 500. These funds may invest in individual stocks or even other mutual funds.

New tactical strategies appear regularly, and they go in and out of style on Wall Street just as the styles in men's ties or women's handbags. So far in 2018, for example, nine-month price momentum has been the top strategy, according to Standard & Poor's Capital IQ. The strategy: buy the stocks and sectors that have gone up the most the past nine months. The worst-performing strategy has been favoring the top-performing stocks by their market capitalization— the number of shares outstanding multiplied by price per share.

In short, the tactical mandate simply tries to go where the opportunities are best, and the risks are least. Unlike the strategic mandate, which typically sticks with passive investments and a relatively static allocation, the tactical mandate can pretty much go anywhere—it could even devote large positions to cash, if conditions are particularly nasty. It may also make use of top-performing actively-managed funds, provided they offer comparatively low costs, good management, and a solid track record. The goal of the tactical mandate is to improve returns on the upside, and reduce losses on the downside. It's an integral part of the Adaptive Portfolio.

CHAPTER 11

THE RISK DIVERSIFIER MANDATE

I skate where the puck is going to be, not where it has been.
- Wayne Gretzky

Back in July of 2010, Dr. Frank Ciampi stepped into his office building in Lorton, Virginia, and noticed something awry. "The floor just outside examination room No. 2—about 10 feet from where Ciampi had been doing paperwork—was littered with small pieces of wood, plaster, and insulation," wrote Paul Duggan of *The Washington Post*. "Upon inspection, more debris lay inside the room. He saw three chunks of stone on the floor that together had formed a rock about the size of a tennis ball, with a glassy-smooth surface. Then he saw a hole about the size of the rock in the tile ceiling, and a tear in the maroon carpet where the rock had landed."

Dr. Ciampi's office had been struck by a meteorite. What are the chances of that? Investors don't need to protect against the highly remote chance of a meteor strike, but they do need to shield against the unexpected. The Risk Diversifier Mandate typically is the smallest section of the Adaptive Portfolio, but it's important. It provides a further counterbalance to the Adaptive Strategic and Adaptive Tactical Mandates by disengaging from the general market cycle. At the same time, it also provides a new source of potential return and risk management.

You may recall from our earlier discussion of Modern Portfolio Theory that mixing investments together that do not move in the same direction—or even those that move inversely from each other—can produce superior returns. The Risk Diversifier mandate attempts to do just that. Alternative or non-correlated asset classes that rise and fall independently of stocks and bonds can mitigate losses and enhance returns in an increasingly volatile investing environment. It is a very active mandate that uses a wider spectrum of asset classes and approaches, with little dependence on market direction. The Risk Diversifier part of the Adaptive Investment Portfolio enhances diversification, risk management, and portfolio protection. We'll detail some of those investments in a bit.

So what kind of investments are we talking about? One type are called liquid alternative investments, or liquid alts in Wall Street jargon. Liquid alts are mutual funds or exchange-traded funds, which doesn't sound terribly revolutionary. But these funds seek to provide investors with diversification and downside protection through alternative investment strategies. While these strategies were pioneered by hedge funds, the mutual fund structure of liquid alternatives provides investors with attractive risk-adjusted growth but, unlike hedge funds, you can buy and sell these funds daily. (Hedge funds typically have a few windows each year when investors can get their money back). Liquid alternatives have historically delivered more stability to investors over various market cycles.

EXAMPLES OF LIQUID ALTERNATIVE STRATEGIES

Nontraditional bond: These funds take unconventional approaches to bond investing, often trying to achieve returns that are uncorrelated with the bond market. "Unconstrained" funds invest with a high degree of flexibility, taking positions in high-yield foreign debt, for example.

Market neutral: Funds that seek to minimize systematic risks born of overexposure to specific sectors, countries, or currencies. They aim to match short positions and long positions within these areas and achieve low beta—which, as you recall, is a measure of volatility relative to an index, such as the Standard & Poor's 500.

Managed futures: These funds invest primarily through derivatives, such as listed and over-the-counter futures, options, swaps, and foreign exchange contracts. When you think of futures, you may think about traders who scan weather reports for information about the Brazilian coffee harvest or frost on the orange crop in Florida. In fact, most futures traders rarely glance out the window, much less inspect soybean fields. Typical managed futures funds are nearly entirely computer-driven, looking for profitable trends—up or down—across all the available futures markets, which range from beans to the Brazilian real.[97] Most managed futures funds use momentum approaches, while others follow mean-reversion strategies—which means they buy or sell in the hopes that

[97] Brazilian currency unit.

an uptrend or downtrend will reverse itself and return to its long-term average.

Buy-Write strategy: This is a hedged equity strategy. An underlying equity allocation is established using ETFs based on fundamental analysis. The strategy creates the hedge by selling covered calls against each of the underlying equity positions. While options tend to make novice investors nervous, covered calls are actually a highly conservative way to invest. The writer (the fund) gets a fee for creating calls, which are the right, but not the obligation, to buy a stock at a set price. In this case, the fund owns the stock, and the biggest risk is that the owner of the call will exercise it and buy the stock at a higher price. In most cases, however, the calls expire worthless, and the call-writing fee becomes a good source of income for the fund. The objective of the strategy is to provide investors with attractive risk-adjusted returns and income while reducing portfolio volatility.

Multialternative: These funds combine different alternative strategies, such as those listed above. They may have fixed allocations to set strategies, or vary their approaches depending on market developments. While not funds of funds[98], they offer many different approaches in one vehicle. As with many multipurpose funds, you have to choose carefully for one run by a team that has expertise in many areas.

---

[98] Fund of funds is an investment strategy of holding a portfolio of other investment funds rather than investing directly in stocks, bonds or other securities. Sometimes referred to as a multi-manager investment.

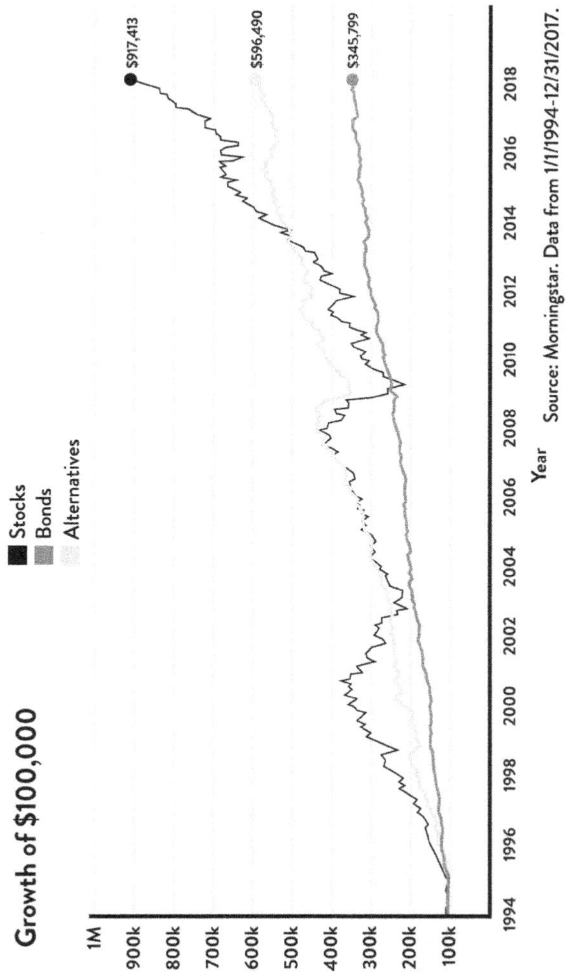

Figure 23.[99] Alternatives have historically delivered more stability to investors over various market cycles. Past returns shown do not guarantee future results. Stocks are represented by the S&P 500 Index, Bonds by the Barclays Aggregated Bond Index, and Alternatives by the Credit Suisse Hedge Fund Index. It is not possible to invest directly in an index.

[99] 361 Capital. "Pursuing a Smoother Investor Experience." 2017. https://361capital.com/financial-advisor/investment-ideas/pursuing-a-smoother/. Accessed 24 October 2018.

SO WHAT'S THE DEAL WITH GOLD?

When I was a young broker at Morgan Stanley, my mentor there asked me this, "So, Michael, how are you going to differentiate yourself from the other guys in the office? How are you going to care for your clients and their money? Are you going to be a stock jockey like everybody else? How are you going to add value as a professional investment manager?" It was a rhetorical question that he proceeded to answer himself. He went on to explain in great detail how he utilized managed futures and precious metals, among other vehicles to help protect clients and improve returns.

Always looking for ways to reduce risk, that is where I got my first exposure to gold, foreign currencies, futures contracts, and energy as instruments to better care for and protect qualified clients.

Gold comes up in the media from time to time, during periods of market duress or with a comment about gold bugs and tinfoil hats. Here is the real deal. Gold has been used as money throughout history, over thousands of years for exchange purposes and as a store of wealth.

People think of gold as a last-chance investment for when the government collapses, and some have even called gold "a direct bet against civilization." And, if you think about it, you'd be better off investing in canned goods and water purifiers if you expect a zombie apocalypse. So, no, you cannot eat gold, drive it, or live in it. And, from an investment standpoint, gold has no earnings and does not pay interest.

The utility of gold is as a currency and a store of value against fiat currencies and the corrosive effects of inflation. (Fiat currencies are those created by central banks by decree. They have no hard assets, such as gold, backing them. Today's money, in the words of Jim Grant, editor of *Grant's Interest Rate Observer*, is money of the mind.)

Along with credit expansion and money creation come consequences in the form of distortions in interest rates and business cycles—even recessions and depressions. Money creation and credit expansion depreciates the value of currency, which is why the U.S. dollar that was worth 100 cents when the Fed was created is now worth less than five cents when adjusted for inflation.

> *If you don't own gold, you know neither history nor economics.*
>
> *Ray Dalio*

Although central banks don't like you to own gold, because it is a direct challenge to the fiat currency, they hold lots of it themselves. According to the World Gold Council, as of September 2018, the United States has 8,133.5 tonnes in gold reserves. Speaking to the World Gold Council for the 2017 winter edition of its gold investor publication, former Federal Reserve Chairman Alan Greenspan said, "I view gold as the primary global currency."

Gold has its place as a risk diversifier as it trades inverse to equities and remains an excellent long-term hedge for disruptive market scenarios. Gold is typically a safe haven asset with strong value properties in deflation scenarios. When looking at crisis periods or during inflationary busts, gold tends to outperform the broad markets and treasuries. Gold has also held up well during crisis periods characterized by declining inflation.

You can own gold in plenty of forms. One way, of course, is to stroll down to a coin dealer and buy a U.S. Eagle, the one-ounce coin produced by the U.S. mint. You'll pay a premium for the coin, because it's a beautiful object and, in most cases, has no dings or scratches on it. This means a lot to coin collectors, but not so much to investors. Your problem then is what to do with it. It's probably not the best idea to keep it in a desk drawer. You can use a safety deposit box, unless you're really worried about the collapse of the government. In that case, you'll have to go old school. Bury it in the backyard in the dead of night and invest in alarm systems and guard dogs.

Fortunately, there are alternatives for investors who think that civilization might muddle through in the next few decades. The biggest breakthrough is gold exchange-traded funds, which own physical gold and sell shares on the stock exchanges. The price goes up and down with the gold market, and the gold itself is kept securely and audited frequently.

Funds that invest in gold mining stocks are another option, albeit one that's more volatile than those that simply track the price of gold. Mark Twain once defined a gold mine as, "A hole in the ground with a liar standing in front of it." While gold equity funds don't invest in the kind of penny stocks that Twain was referring to, mining stocks can indeed be volatile.

Here's why: Suppose you own an ounce of gold that, conveniently for those who like easy math, cost you $1,000. If the price rises to $1,500, you've made 50 percent on your investment. Now suppose you own a gold mine, and can pull gold out of the ground for $900 an ounce. If gold rises to $1,500, your earnings have risen from $100 an ounce to $600 an ounce—a 500 percent increase.

All but the most enthusiastic gold investors tend to recommend a relatively small position in gold for your portfolio: basically, as insurance against inflation and other catastrophes. If you make a huge amount of money in gold, the world you inhabit will probably not be a very nice place to live—but at least you'll have some money.

CHAPTER 12

KEEPING THE BALANCE

Moderate in order to taste the joys of life in abundance.
- Epicurus

Another component of the Adaptive Investment Portfolio is rebalancing, which is the process of returning your portfolio to the original alignment and mandate allocations determined by your age, risk profile, and time horizon as well as goals. Rebalancing is the methodology that systemically buys low and sells high without your emotions getting in the way.

Intellectually, we all know we should buy low and sell high, but that's often easier said than done. Rebalancing forces you to sell a portion of your winning investments (selling high) and reinvest that sum in your losers (buying low). As a simple example, suppose you wanted to have 60 percent of the strategic sleeve of your portfolio in stocks and 40 percent in bonds. After a rip-snorting bull market, you now have 70 percent in stocks and 30 percent bonds. That's great. But you now have more risk in your portfolio, because you have 10 percent more in stocks and 10 percent less in bonds. To rebalance, you'll have to sell the 10 percent increase in your stock holdings and reinvest the proceeds in your bond portfolio, bringing it back into balance with the original allocation.

By rebalancing the Adaptive Investment Portfolio, we make sure that your overall asset allocation remains where you want it to be. For some people, rebalancing is counter-intuitive and challenging, as it requires one to sell winners and buy more of the losing positions. This is how the natural herding instinct affects our bias. Rebalancing is an important discipline that keeps your portfolio risk exposure in line with your risk tolerance.

Rebalancing can be done in different ways and at different times. For example, some advisors may recommend rebalancing at a pre-determined timetable such as every quarter or once per year. Another approach is to rebalance your portfolio based on a percentage change in your allocation. Let's consider how you might rebalance your overall Adaptive Investment Portfolio. As an example, the three mandates may break down like this:

1. Adaptive Strategic: 70 percent
2. Adaptive Tactical: 20 percent
3. Adaptive Risk Diversifier: 10 percent

If you had chosen a 10 percent threshold for change and you saw your Adaptive Strategic move to 80 percent, the Adaptive Tactical move to 40 percent and your Adaptive risk Diversifier move to 5 percent would trigger the portfolio to rebalance back to 70, 20, and 10 percent, respectively.

As you might expect, the returns of the rebalanced portfolio are less volatile because the rebalanced portfolio's allocations are maintained at target levels.

Portfolio allocations and rebalancing targets may change over time, due to life events such as the birth of a child or the approach of retirement. You have to reset your portfolio to your personal situation.

With a well-diversified portfolio and strategy, at some point you will have positions that are losing and, simultaneously, you will have positions that are winning. That is the whole point of asset and strategy diversification, and what smooths out the volatility in your portfolio.

ADJUSTMENTS

Investment portfolios need care and watering too. Once you've created your investment portfolio (or had one created for you), don't just set it and forget it. When markets shift and cycles change, it is necessary to execute allocation and exposure changes to each mandate. These disciplined adjustments, not market timing, can rapidly modify an investment strategy for changing market conditions in order to achieve superior risk-adjusted returns. Markets can change quickly, so it's important to regularly check in on your portfolio as well as any changes to your personal situation. A review of your portfolio when markets are up can be a lot of fun, while doing that work while markets are falling may be, well...not as fun.

Here are a few questions to ask yourself at least once a year:

1. Have your objectives or time horizon changed?
2. Have economic or market conditions changed? Different investment instruments come in and out of favor in different points of the market cycle, and your portfolio should reflect that.
3. Is anything not working? While not everything in each mandate is meant to increase in price at the same time, some strategies may have strategic justification. However, if none can be found, then it may need to be removed.

A WORD ABOUT TAXES

As with any investment strategy, the Adaptive Investment Portfolio can generate taxes when you move in and out of positions. Taxes are one of the greatest costs to portfolio performance. Some years, you could have taxable losses and gains in your portfolio. The Adaptive Investment Portfolio may be more tax efficient than a buy-and-hold strategy, although that will depend on many factors. I am not an accountant and I do not give tax advice. I am simply making the point that the way you structure and manage your investment portfolio, particularly for high net-worth individuals, can help you keep more of your money and ultimately improve your investment performance.

Bear in mind that not all capital gains are treated equally and the tax rate from your investments can vary dramatically. Being aware of the taxes that affect you and your investments is crucial. Please familiarize yourself with a few of them and consult your CPA or tax professional.

- **Short-term capital gains**: These do not benefit from any special tax rate; they are taxed at the same rate as your ordinary income. If you sell an asset you have held for one year or less, you will be subject to tax on any profit you make.
- **Long-term capital gains**: If you hold your investment for longer than one year, you can benefit from a reduced tax rate on your profits.
- **Capital losses**: If you lose money on your investments rather than making a profit, you can use those losses to reduce your taxes. The IRS allows you to match up your gains and losses for any given year to determine your "net" capital gain or loss. If you end up with a net loss, you can use up to $3,000 per

year of your capital losses to reduce your taxable income. Any additional losses can be carried-forward into future years, to offset either capital gains or another $3,000 in ordinary income.

That's why a big part of the Adaptive Investment Portfolio depends on you: what your goals are, what risks you are willing to take, and how your situation changes. You'll have to make adjustments to the Adaptive Investment Portfolio, and that's what financial planning is for. Being prepared and well-armed with a clear vision of what you want and how you want to get there, the Adaptive Investment Portfolio will give you a well-diversified strategy that adapts to dynamic market conditions. By allocating your capital in these three areas, rebalancing periodically, and keeping an eye on taxes, you have an inherently adaptive portfolio that can weather market volatility, no matter the economic conditions. The key to a good night's sleep and peace of mind is knowing exactly what you are invested in and why you are invested.

IN CONCLUSION

We are living in the most incredible time in history. Things are good and I am optimistic about the future. With advancements in medicine and science, our life expectancy is the longest it has ever been. Millions of people around the world now live to be well over the age of ninety. Despite the seemingly nonstop news coverage of global conflicts, there has actually never been a more peaceful time on earth. Technology has never been better and we have virtually unlimited information available at our fingertips. Our access to food, travel, and entertainment has never been better.

It is also a time of great change and ever-increasing complexity. With stock market indices at all-time record highs, we are now in the longest bull market in history, and it is likely that we are closer to the top of the cycle than we are to the bottom. To ensure that the financial security of our futures and that of our families remains bright, our portfolios need to be able to adapt to the rapidly-changing global economic landscape.

As Charles Darwin said, "It is not the strongest of the species that survives, nor the most intelligent. It is the one that is most adaptable to change."

The Adaptive Investment Portfolio is your way to adapt to the ever-changing financial landscape.

CONCLUSION

KEY TERMS

Active management: An investment strategy that attempts to create excess returns with the goal of outperforming and investment benchmark index through the recognitions, anticipation and exploitation of market inefficiencies and short term trends.

Alternative assets: An asset that is not one of the conventional investment types, such as stocks, bonds, or currencies. Alternative investments include private equity, hedge funds, managed futures, real estate, commodities, and derivative contracts.

Alpha: A risk-adjusted measure of the "excess return" provided by an investment compared with a benchmark. Alpha can be positive, negative, or zero.

Beta: The beta of an investment indicates whether the investment is more or less volatile than the market as whole.

Bear market: A market where securities prices fall and widespread pessimism causes the stock markets to fall and become self-fulfilling. Generally, a downturn of 20 percent or more from a market peak is considered entry into a bear market.

Black box: A computer model used by a manager to produce returns.

Bull market: A market where securities prices are rising or are expected to rise by 20% or more, usually for a period of months or years. The term "bull market" is most often used to refer to the stock market but can be applied to anything that is traded, such as bonds, real estate, currencies, and commodities.

Buy side: The investment part of the financial services industry, including asset managers, institutional investors, hedge funds and retail investors.

Call option: A contract giving the buyer the right to buy an asset at a given price within a given time period.

Closed fund: A fund that is not open to new investors. Managers usually close funds so they do not dilute returns by being too big for their markets. Sometimes closed funds will allow existing investors to put in more money (a condition known as "soft closed").

Collateralized Debt Obligation (CDO): A security that bundles together a number of bonds or loans and then slices them up into tranches, based on their risk.

Correlation: Is a statistical measure explaining the strength and direction of how two securities or portfolios move in relation to each other. The value of a correlation can move between -1 and +1. The closer the correlation between two securities is to +1, the stronger the relationship and the more they will tend to move in the same direction. The closer the correlation is to -1, the stronger the relationship and the more the two securities will tend to move in opposite directions. If the correlations is close to zero, the two securities will tend not to have a strong relationship. The Alternative assets and risk diversifiers are often described as uncorrelated assets.

Cumulative Return: Total amount an investment has gained (or lost) over time, expressed as a percentage. It is important to consider the context of time and comparable investments when looking at cumulative return.

Derivatives: Instruments that derive their value from that of another asset. Examples are futures contracts, options, or swaps.

Drawdown: A term used to describe the peak-to-trough decline during a specific recorded period of an investment, fund, or commodity security.

Emerging markets: The financial markets of developing countries, such as China, Egypt, and Mexico.

Equity risk premium: The excess return, over bonds, payable to shareholders to compensate them for the greater risk involved.

Expense ratio: A mutual fund's annual operating costs expressed as a percentage of average net assets.

Fat tail: The tendency for returns to be more extreme than normal (bell curve) distribution would suggest. This creates a skewness or kurtosis.

Leverage: The use of borrowed money to enhance returns. A fund that is three times levered has borrowed three times more than it originally had as investors' capital.
Long-only: The way that money has traditionally been managed. Investors buy assets they believe will rise in price.

Long-short: A strategy that combines long positions with short positions. The resulting portfolio gives some protection against market falls and takes advantage of a manager's stock-picking skills.

Macro funds: Fund that take big positions in share, bond, or currency markets based on their views of how economic trends will develop.

Managed account: A separate account run on behalf of high net-worth individuals. The main appeal for wealthy investors is the access to professional money managers, a high degree of customization, and greater tax efficiencies in a fee-based product.
Market neutral funds: Funds that try to eliminate stock market risk. They consist of equal long and short positions. Provided the manager picks the right stocks, the fund will rise in value, regardless of the market's direction.

Net assets: The closing market value of a fund's assets minus its liabilities.

Sell side: The part of the financial industry that is involved in the creation, promotion, and sale of stocks, bonds, foreign exchange, and other financial instruments.

Short selling: A strategy that bets on falling prices. The investor borrows the asset (at a cost), sells it in the market, and then hopes to buy it back at a lower price.

Skewness: Asymmetry in a statistical distribution. In a normal distribution, a bell curve applies with numbers evenly distributed on either side of the average. Skewness can be quantified to define the extent to which a distribution differs from a normal distribution.

Standard deviation: In finance, standard deviation is a statistical measurement that is used to quantify the amount of variation, or dispersion, within a set of data values. When applied to the annual rate of return of an investment, it sheds light on the historical volatility of that investment.

Stop loss: A tactic used to limit loss on a position. A stop-loss order is placed to activate the sale of a security when it reaches a certain price.

Technical analysis: Using chart patterns of previous price movements to predict future changes in asset price.

Turnover: An indication of a fund's trading activity. Turnover represents the lesser of aggregate purchases or sales of securities divided by average net assets.

Value-at-risk: A measure of the riskiness of a portfolio, usually relating to the maximum loss in one day's trade.

Variance: A measurement of the spread between numbers in a data set. The variance measures how far each number in the set is from the mean.

Volatility: The size of fluctuations of an asset price or portfolio over time as measured by the standard deviation of logarithmic returns.

ABOUT THE AUTHOR

MICHAEL P. ERNST is the founder and CEO of Ernst & Co. Wealth Management, LLC a fee-only, Registered Investment Advisor (RIA). Michael started his career at Morgan Stanley over 24 years ago where he had a mentor that was a Barron's Top 100 Advisor and an investment advisor to Bill Gross of Janus Capital (previously Pimco). Learning early in his career from one of the industries most sophisticated and successful professionals helped develop his expertise on how to best help his clients navigate market cycles and meet their most important financial goals with specific risk management, asset diversification and growth strategies. Michael currently works with high net worth individuals and families in Manhattan Beach, California where he lives with his wife, Jessica, and sons, Adam and Ethan.

IMPORTANT DISCLOSURE INFORMATION

Michael P. Ernst is the founder of Ernst & Co. Wealth Management, LLC, offering wealth management services in California. Certain portions of the book may reflect positions and or recommendations as of a specific prior date, and may no longer be reflective of current positions and/or recommendations for various reasons, including but not limited to, regulatory changes. No reader should assume that the book serves as the receipt of, or substitute for, personalized advice from Mr. Ernst or Ernst & Co. Wealth Management, LLC or from any other investment professional. Please remember that different types of investments involve varying degrees of risk. Therefore, it should not be assumed that any future performance of any specific investment, investment product, or investment strategy (including the investments and/or investment strategies referenced in this book), or any of the book's non-investment related content, will be profitable, prove successful, or be applicable to any individual's specific situation. Should a reader have any questions regarding the applicability of any portion of the book's content to his/her individual situations, the reader is encouraged to consult with a professional financial advisor of his/her choosing.

An actively managed portfolio cannot assure a profit or protect against loss. Inherent limitations and market conditions may affect the performance of a portfolio. There is no guarantee that an actively managed portfolio can produce greater returns or experience smaller losses than a portfolio that uses a buy-and-hold strategy. High turnover rates within a portfolio may increase transactions costs and taxable capital gains. Indexes are unmanaged, and investors are not able to invest directly into any index.

Investors should be aware that there are risks inherent in all investments, such as fluctuations or loss in investment principal. With any investment vehicle, past performance is not a guarantee of future results.

Materials discussed herein are meant for general illustration and/or information purposes only. Please note that individual situations can vary. Therefore, the information should be relied upon only when coordinated with individual professional financial advice.

The S&P 500 is an unmanaged index comprised of five hundred widely held securities considered to be representative of the stock market in general.

Sector investing may involve a greater degree of risk than investments with broader diversification.

Investments in real estate have various risks, including the possible lack of liquidity and devaluation based on adverse economic and regulatory changes. As a result, the values of real estate may fluctuate, resulting in the value at sale being more or less than the original price paid.

Global or international investing involves special risks, such as currency fluctuations over short periods of time, and may be affected by unpredictable international monetary and political policies. The market for commodities is subject to varying regulatory regimes, and concentrated investing may lead to higher price volatility. In addition, investing in commodities often involves international investing in emerging markets, which involve significant risks.

www.ingramcontent.com/pod-product-compliance
Lightning Source LLC
Chambersburg PA
CBHW031934190326
41519CB00007B/525
* 9 7 8 1 7 3 2 8 9 4 6 0 0 *